Blood Trail

Reflections on hunting and life

Jeff Krogstad

Books by Jeff Krogstad:

<u>Fiction</u>
Death on Disappointment Mountain
Fair Game

<u>Nonfiction</u>
From Slavery To Freedom: A personal reading of the Exodus story
New Wineskins: A commentary on the gospel of Luke
Wait for the Lightning: A fresh look at Genesis 1-12

Find all Jeff's books and more at
jeffkrogstad.com

*For my brothers
who have lived these words*

Contents

Fall

Blood Trail

The pine needles had been scuffed, as if someone planted the toe of a boot and shifted their foot just a little. I stopped for a moment in the darkness. The bright beam from my flashlight focused on that spot and I stood motionless, trying to peel back time. Where have we walked so far? Did any of us step here? We came into this clearing back there, walked all around the bait, and over there by the treestand. Right now my three brothers were casting about a few steps to the east, on the bear's habitual trail, looking for sign. None of us had stepped on these scuffed pine needles.

With a little imagination, I traced a line from the bait, over the scuffed needles, into the darkness. It made sense. The line started at the bait and moved away from Darin's stand, into the safety of the dark. There was almost an opening in the brush there. That branch might be freshly broken.

I moved toward the opening, and soon found leaves blocking my view. Down on all fours and I crawled, like Alice down the rabbit hole, into the darkness. I examined every pine needle, every leaf in my path. Ten or twelve feet later I found it.

"Blood here!"

My brothers gathered quickly.

We were bowhunting for black bears in the Pine Island State Forest of northern Minnesota, deep in a peat bog we'd hunted off and on since we were children. Most of our lives we had come here for ruffed grouse, but the last several years we'd taken to bowhunting for the black bears that live nearly invisible in the north woods. Darin, the youngest and the tallest of us, arrowed one that evening. He figured it was a small two year old. Darin wasn't sure of the hit. He thought it might be a little far back. Now we faced the daunting task of finding the blood trail in the dark and (hopefully) finding a dead bear at the end of the trail.

The dark smear of blood I found was ten inches up the trunk of a small tree. The dog hair poplars were thick here, about four feet tall, trunks a half inch thick. Pushing through them the bear had smeared blood on the gray trunks. A heart or lung hit would be pouring out blood by this point. The blood smeared on the trees, little blood on the ground, meant that the hit was too far back. This would be a difficult trail.

The only way to track through the little trees was on hands and knees. Every so often the brush opened up. Then we stood up and strained our eyes, lanterns and flashlights held at odd angles, straining to see blood drops against the dark pine needles. The trail would descend into the poplars again and we crawled into the dark.

None of us carried a weapon more lethal than a hunting knife. We were bowhunting. What good is archery in the dark? Black bears are timid creatures. They flee from people. In my whole childhood, I'd only ever seen two in the wild, each for a few seconds as they ran away. I'd seen their tracks faint in the sand on the roadway or in the mud at the edge of the Lost River. I'd marveled at the trees they marked, claw marks higher than I could reach shredding the bark on old white pines. I'd even seen a hole torn and chewed in the side of an old hunting cabin where a bear had gone in looking for leftovers. But I had rarely seen the timid bears themselves until we started hunting them. Now I was tracking one on the ground, and a wounded one at that. My brothers followed me single file through the brush.

Pushing forward through the latest patch of willows, as I limped on three legs, one hand holding the flashlight, I wondered about the wisdom of pushing a potentially gut-shot bear.

At that instant I heard movement in the dark. Fifteen yards in front of me. Something bigger than a raccoon moved through the brush, moving (thank goodness!) away from me. I backed off, and we decided to mark the spot. We'd find our way out in the dark with a compass, and come back in the morning.

A blood trail demands everything you have to give. You're not here for entertainment. The weight of the blood, drop by drop, cries out from the ground in crimson words, telling of your responsibility: you have taken a life. At one end of the trail is a wounded animal, bleeding out its life, desperate to escape the wound, desperate for a den, a bed, a place of safety. Drop by drop its life drains onto the ground. At the other end of the trail is one who was a hunter, now a tracker seeking to redeem the shot, to vindicate the wound by recovering the animal. These two are connected by blood and by a few stray marks on the earth. The blood trail.

Reading a blood trail is like reading pictographs, like reading the meaning of geese on the sky, like reading a fleeting expression that drifts across your lover's face. There is meaning there to be found, but it takes skill, practice, compassion, and imagination to understand it.

I have followed Jesus all my adult life. In childhood I knew him, and our paths crossed from time to time. I began to follow his trail in earnest as a young man. As an adult, I have strained to understand the marks of his blood drained out for me. He moves out ahead of me like a ghostly shape through the trees, like a buck wounded to the heart, like a gut shot bear. On hands and knees sometimes, often in the dark, limping on three legs, flashlight in one hand, I follow.

Where is he leading me? I want to go back to Sunday School and say, "It's not true! You told us that he would walk with us and talk with us. We sang, 'What a Friend We Have In Jesus' and it all sounded like a sunny afternoon at the beach." But following Jesus is a blood trail. It is a desperate quest to make my way through the darkness, holding to the truth. His life is my life, his death is mine as well. We are connected by blood.

I could leave his trail. I could go back to my recliner, open a beer and catch the fourth quarter of the Vikings game. He would still be out here, bleeding in the dark for me. Drop by drop, I follow.

Church people are not good at acknowledging the difficulties, the challenges of following Jesus. Strange, because the New Testament talks about these challenges on nearly every page. Rejoice in your sufferings. Count it all joy when you experience trials. I came not to bring peace, but a sword. Blessed are you when men insult you and speak all manner of falsehood about you. Our sermons and our songs are full of the joy of following Jesus but we do a poor job of talking about the difficulties.

It was like a breath of fresh air to me when I ran across this quote in a book called, appropriately enough, *Stuck!* by Terry Walling:

> *A new Christ follower often consistently gets answers from God and feels the results of being chased and romanced by God... We sense his presence and its reassurance, and build our lives on the promise that he will never leave us or forsake us ...*
>
> *At an undefined point, it sometimes appears that God begins to step back, almost as if to abandon the Christ follower. His closeness seems to vanish.*
>
> *It is not betrayal, but God beginning to build depth into our relationship with him. He*

chased us, and he will continue his pursuit of us.
But Christ followers now begin to see our role
also as pursuers of God. Like lovers in pursuit of
each other, our pursuit of God now meets his
ongoing pursuit of us.

We came back to the trail as the sunrise filtered through the thick pines. This time, in daylight, we brought a pistol. A blood trail looks so strange in daylight. Remembering the night before, you feel like adults watching a children's game of blind man's bluff or pin the tail on the donkey. It's a little embarrassing to remember the darkness and the adrenaline.

The trail hadn't moved overnight. We found our marker and started following. This time Darin took the lead. Another hundred and fifty yards brought us into a clearing where a few giant cedars towered into the gray sky. At the base of one of these giants, like a bit of black lint tucked up against a log, we found the bear, gasping, nearly spent, with just enough life to snarl and feint one last time. One well-placed shot ended his agony and our pursuit.

With bloody hands, we half carried and half dragged him out through the brush, over the long trail back to the road. Like Joseph of Arimathea placing a lifeless body in a rocky tomb, we lifted him into the back of Darin's Chevy.

Two bears for four hunters that year. We butchered them in camp and divided the meat. Months later, sitting at the supper table, I carved a bear roast for my family. My daughters were convinced that bear meat was the best kind of meat in the world. They loved it. Over the last few bites, I tried to explain things to Erica, who was six years old at the time. "We shot the bear, and we took good care of the meat, and now we eat it. That bear's meat feeds us, makes us strong. Our life costs something. It costs the life of the bear. So it's important what we do with our life."

There was something deeper here that I couldn't explain to her, or even to myself. I felt the truth of it deep down, like a sliver in my gut that kept pulling me back to the memory of that night on hands and knees in the woods. My life and the bear's life were intertwined. The trail of his blood smeared on the dog-hair popples, spattered across the pine needles, tied us together like a dull red cord from heart to heart. This is the critical message that most of us miss as we drift through life, eating artificial food wrapped in plastic and paper and pink styrofoam. Your life comes at a price, and the price must be paid in blood. Don't miss it.

Hunting Alone

I know hunters that never hunt alone. They hunt waterfowl, mostly, with partners and dogs, decoys strung out on the marsh in front of them, shotguns at the ready. They whisper and chuckle together in the blind while they wait for a flight of bluebills to clear the horizon.

Some of them are deer hunters. They hunt during rifle season, a dozen in camp together, blaze orange jackets walking down the scrubby field edges in a line to drive the deer to the orange men posting at the far end. They meet at the far end of the field and swap stories of shots and misses and they collect a buck, or a couple does, off the frozen ground and move on to the next piece of land.

I have never been much of a duck hunter, and while I have tried deer hunting in packs, I have nearly always hunted alone. I may camp with hunting partners. I may even walk out to the woods with them. But only rarely do I actually hunt with someone else.

Hunting alone, each hunt is a test. Can I find the stand in the dark? Can I discipline my feet, my hands, my breathing? Can I stifle that cough? Can I stay awake and aware and not be taken by surprise? I sit alone on stand, or I still hunt through the woods and face myself. I think through the what-ifs. I bring last night's argument with my wife and spread it out on the stand with me, rethinking the conflict, dealing with the tension, second-guessing my actions. I carry work problems in my pack with my gloves and granola bars and ponder them while I sit. Occasionally I force myself to be in the moment, to let all the other tensions go and just be the hunter. These moments are the best times.

November of 2000 I hunted the rifle season in western North Dakota. I had drawn a mule deer doe tag. Two feet of early snow blanketed the badlands. The snow kept many semi-desert hunters close to the roads, but I grew up in the woods of northern Minnesota. While they griped about the blizzard, I strapped on my snowshoes and waded out across the broad coulees where drifts stood ten or fifteen feet deep. That long Saturday I walked about ten miles up and down the draws, seeing lots of sign but no deer.

From the earliest beams of sunrise through the dazzling morning and into a gray afternoon, I wrestled two enemies in my mind.

First and most important, my father lay dying seven hours to the east. A squamous cell carcinoma had metastasized in his elbow, then his armpit, and the surgeon said it had entered his lymph system. Just shy of eighty, the man who taught me about hunting and about deer and about solitude was now teaching me about dying. All that fall I'd been road tripping to visit him on my days off. I'd watched him letting go, little by little, and we both knew we were approaching an end. The knowledge hung like a lead ball in my chest. Though Dad had always hunted whitetails in the forests with his open-sighted .280, I knew he would approve of me carrying a .30-06 with a scope and looking for mule deer in these coulees. I hoped to have a chance to tell him about the day.

The second lead weight in my chest came from the fact that at least in terms of meat, I was a poor hunter. I had come to a crisis of faith about it. It had been many years since I brought home venison. I loved to hunt, and I talked constantly about it and spent many hours at it. But lately my family ate beef, not venison.

For a guy who grew up among hunters, manhood and meat get all tangled up sometimes. Months of reflecting on my father's life and my upbringing brought into stark relief just how critical it was for me to hunt, and to hunt well.

As the day wore on and a cold front moved down the Missouri River valley, a sneaking suspicion grew in my mind that my hunting habit had become an idol. I stood on a knoll glassing the empty hillsides and wondered if God was preventing me from shooting a deer so that I would turn away from my idolatry, back to him.

That begged another question. What if God showed up in a burning tumbleweed out there in the hills and told me to give up hunting? Could I obey? Was that, in fact, the test he was putting before me? Maybe I was like Abraham, called to lay my beloved son Isaac, or at least my love of hunting, on the altar and sacrifice it.

The thought tore at my guts. Who would I be if I was not a hunter? The last five or six years Dad had pretty much given up hunting. It had gone bland for him, like food goes tasteless during chemo, and he just didn't show much interest. Two, maybe three years now he hadn't even bought a license. For myself, I couldn't imagine letting go.

The clouds grew darker. They hunched over the tops of the hills like a heavy pillow descending to smother the day. A few stray snowflakes raced like bullets on the driving northwest wind. It would be dark in an hour, and I had two miles to go back to the car. My snowshoes made teardrop prints across the drifts as I worked my way down the slope, across the wide flood plain, and began to climb the far side, the wind in my right eye the whole way. As I trudged, I carried on a monologue with God, whispering my words and hoping he'd speak out loud in response.

"I have a sneaking suspicion that you want me to give up hunting."

Silence except for the pt - pt - pt of ice pellets on the wind hitting my coat.

"I wonder if that's why I've brought home no meat for so many years. Are you patiently waiting for me to give up this idol worship?"

I crossed the channel where, in spring, water rushed through the bottom. Now it was dry, buried under several feet of fresh powder. Still no voice from the clouds. Climbing out, I continued.

"Or is this the way you've created me? Did you make me to be a hunter? And even if you did, am I honoring you in how much time and effort I put into hunting? Is it really idol worship, or am I just living out your design for me?"

The wind bit into my right eyebrow as I began to work my way up the slope. More snowflakes rode that wind now, and the far hillsides were starting to look unfocused as the snow picked up and the sun went down. I came to a moment of decision.

"Jesus, you know that if you tell me to do something I'll do it. I made that commitment long ago. So," and I physically stopped on the hillside for a moment before plunging in, afraid of what I was about to say. "If you tell me you want me to stop hunting, and if you make it absolutely clear, like a two-by-four to the forehead, I'll do it. I'll give up hunting." The words clanged like a harsh bell in my heart.

I waited. The snow kept falling.

I moved up the slope until I crested a low ridge. This ridge rose to my right, up toward the plateau where my car was parked. I'd be climbing this ridge through the twilight, step by step the rest of the way up. I paused there, above the coulee bottom but far below the shelf above. I looked around, and my heart was empty. My guts held a vague fear that I would never hear an answer, that I would limp along for years not knowing what was right, not knowing who I was or who I should be.

Far off to the southwest, down the coulee, I saw something moving on the hillside. Through the binoculars I could see a herd of about a dozen mulies working their way down the slope toward the brush in the canyon at the bottom. I knew that bottom, and I could see exactly where they would go.

They would come down into the trees on the south branch of that creek and work their way westward, out of the wind, down toward the Missouri River bottom where they would feed sheltered from the bitter wind. To get there, they would pass through an open spot where the north and south branches of the creek joined up about a half mile from me.

Twenty minutes of twilight left, maybe less. The deer dropped down into the creek bottom where I could not see them. I started running on those snowshoes, running toward an ambush where the creeks came together. I knew I had just a few minutes before the lead doe emerged from the south branch into the wide grassy spot. I had to be in place before that. With each snowshoe step my breath came in great gasps. I inhaled lungfuls of cold air and more than a few dry snowflakes.

Seventy yards this side of the creek, a line of small trees stood out across the slope. I ran until I could slide down behind one of those trees. I knew I'd need a good place to rest the rifle after that run. My heart pounded against my ribs like the dull side of an axehead. I leveled the rifle on a branch and tried to breathe.

Waiting. Where were they? Nothing.

Thirty seconds later, like a ray of sunshine through the thick clouds, that first doe came out of the brush into the open. Single file they came, one after the other. I let the first four clear the draw, then chose the biggest doe, centered my crosshairs on her chest, and fired. She went down in the snow and the rest of the herd bolted back into the canyon.

It took me two hours to drag her up the slope to my Oldsmobile. I grinned nearly the whole time, partly for the venison. Mostly for the answer. Somehow in the face of my doubts, in the silence of the snowstorm, in the unlikely timing of my monologue and desperation and openness, God spoke. He created me to hunt.

Is it possible for me to make hunting into an idol? Of course it is. But he wasn't calling me to abandon this love; rather, I had a deep sense, toiling up that slope, that he was calling me to bring my love for hunting to the table, to fold it into my greater love for him, to let those two great loves grow together, to find that he loves hunting with me.

I finally got back to the car and got the doe loaded in the trunk. I planned to hang the carcass for a day, then cut up the meat myself. I was looking forward to the butchering, to cutting and wrapping and labeling each roast for the freezer.

But the next evening my brother called. Dad had slipped away.

In the view from years later, the synchronicity is clearer. Even as Dad taught me about solitude and death, God was leading me into my father's tracks, into my identity as a hunter, into the quiet where his Spirit broods in tree stands and coulees.

I began to learn that day to trust that God is not afraid of my love of the wild world. He loves it, too. I hunt alone because in those solitary hours, I begin to hear his voice.

Etching Our Names

The alarm breaks through and I wake like a fish being pulled reluctantly from deep water. All I want is to stay in the depths. It is an early September hunt, so the days are longer than the nights. By the time we get back to camp in the dark, cook, eat, and clean up, it's late. When the alarm goes off two hours before sunrise, we groan. It's day four of our hunt, and we're all short on sleep.

This particular day I'm planning to hunt with my brother Les. We were up even later than usual poring over maps and planning today's hunt. We're in the badlands of North Dakota, hunting on foot through twenty-five square miles of roadless country. This area is an island of peace in the middle of an oil boom. Laying atop a ridge glassing for mulies, we can see three drilling rigs on the horizon north, east, and southwest. As we walk back to camp in the dusk, each rig looks like a carnival midway with towers and bright lights. Early mornings, we hear the jake brakes on the trucks three miles away up on Magpie Road when they slow down to avoid a deer or a cow. This is cattle country, and herds of angus and black whiteface cows range through the hills.

The cows hover like flies around the waterholes. A few brave ones wander down into the canyons. They can make a routine walk to an early morning stand a little exciting. Like yesterday, when Les surprised an angus bull sleeping in the brush alongside the trail. It woke as he passed and emerged from the brush like a crazed bulldozer, bleary and disoriented. It stood twenty feet from him, staring and puffing, as if trying to remember where it was and what this camouflaged human might be doing there. Finally Les just circled up the hillside around the poor bull.

Most often the cattle are just an annoyance, like when my nephew Chris planned to hunt up a canyon the other day. Just as he arrived, a herd of two dozen cows trailed up that very canyon, ensuring that the deer would vacate the area and that Chris could not hunt without creating a noticeable stir among the half-wild cows.

There are predators here as well. Coyotes are commonplace, and they seem to be prospering. Lately rabbits are rare, and we speculate about what else a hungry coyote might find in these badlands.

Our first day out I walked a deep canyon, following a dusty trail cut by the hooves of hundreds of cows over the years. Early that morning, five hundred miles to the east, Darin had rolled into my driveway at 3 a.m. So I was already short on sleep.

As I followed the cow trail that first afternoon I contemplated finding a shady spot to settle in under a juniper for an hour's nap before the deer were likely to emerge. Then I noticed mountain lion prints on the trail. The prints were crisp and well-defined in the dust. A day old? Ten minutes? My nap could wait.

Back to the morning of day four. Darin has been hunting a ridge to the north of camp. Chris, enjoying his first badlands hunt, is getting comfortable in the maze of canyons to the east. Les and I will head west and see what we can find in the long, deep canyon and its network of finger ridges and coulees that drains off toward Whitetail Creek to the north.

But first comes the predawn ritual of getting ready. We fumble for socks and rummage in Rubbermaid totes to find our camo. We stumble around the trees in the little creek bottom where we're camped. We look like coal miners, headlamps strapped to our foreheads. Someone thinks to light a Coleman lantern and hang it on a tree branch to help us all out. Darin drags assorted bagels and cream cheese out of the cooler. Les pulls out hamburger buns and dried venison for sandwiches to carry along, as we don't plan to be back during daylight today. I put water on the camp stove for coffee. A quarter hour later, we're completing our preparations. Day packs bulge with water, food, maps, and the other "just in case" items.

Water is the most critical thing we carry. In this dry land, the arid air sucks the moisture from lips and eyes and nostrils. You can find a puddle here and there where the deer go for water, but you wouldn't want to drink it yourself. Even the relatively clean water in the cow tanks has a red caste that makes us shy away from using it for anything besides washing.

Stars are fading. A waning crescent moon hangs next to Orion in the eastern sky. Darin picks up his bow and fades up the hill into the darkness. Chris leaves by a slightly different route. Les and I recheck our gear. Don't forget your binoculars. We turn off the lantern before we head up the opposite slope into the fading dark.

As the sky grows lighter behind us, we feel the pressure of time. We want to be well into the west canyon by daylight. Les sets a Daytona 500 pace, speedwalking up the hill through the red prairie grass and past the fenceposts that loom up in the dimness and disappear as we pass. He's walked this trail several times. I've been here only twice, so I follow his lead. Down and around the hillside, into a stand of junipers and then onto a wide shelf. Back into the trees, plunging down a cow trail used so long it's worn down two and a half feet into the hillside. Juniper branches close over our heads and tug at our packs.

We emerge from the trees onto a white flatness that is characteristic of the badlands. This white dirt, similar to the material used inside drywall, is soft and a little slippery when wet. In the rain it oozes like a glacier, then it dries hard as concrete. We go over a little saddle between two small buttes. If it was light, or if we slowed enough to lean over and inspect the ground, we could see skid marks, tracks four feet long where deer have tried to negotiate the slope when it's wet. I can't imagine those graceful beasts sliding breakneck down the slope.

We're moving too fast in the dim light to stop for tracks. The far side of the saddle opens out into a knife-like ridge. We cross over a pathway perhaps four feet wide with sheer drops of a hundred feet on either side. Climb up the far slope using the old petrified stump for a foothold, and up on top. Follow the top of the ridge another hundred yards, avoiding the noisy skeletons of old sage bushes along the way. Then down a series of steep eroded slides.

I'm thankful we're running a little late now so that we can see the ground under our feet. All the same, the growing light pushes us to move fast, even on these treacherous hillsides. The slope drops at forty-five degrees in places, and only by wedging your heels into the narrow washouts can you climb down without sliding. Sliding on these slopes can be disastrous. Here and there the white powdery rock gives way to bentonite, a crumbly clay soil that clumps up into little chunks that act like ball bearings under your feet. Then a little ways later the ground is covered by bits of baked clay tile called scoria. Their sharp edges chime and clink like little warning bells under your feet.

As we stop on the last level ground before the valley floor, a doe emerges from the brush sixty yards away. She's seen us working our way down the hill and stands with those characteristic mule deer ears like radar dishes tuned to our frequency. She stomps and stares as we stand frozen. Our tags are bucks only, so she's in no danger from us. She can, however, alert every deer for a half mile to our presence. We look at each other with wry smiles. "Guess we better just keep going." Thankfully she only snorts at us once before bounding off when we begin to climb down the last few feet.

Finally we are down off the ridge, into the bottom of the valley. We cross through the deep, dry channel cut by flood waters, then up the far side, to climb a knob that rises forty feet. The top of this tiny hill is covered with broken bits of shale, like fragments of shattered flowerpots across the whole hilltop. We ease carefully, placing one foot gently at a time, trying hard not to make a lot of noise. Lying in the wind atop this little knoll we focus our binoculars in all directions, trying to see into the shadows under each bush, comparing each branch to the shape of an antler. Nothing. As the sun rises above the eastern horizon, Les spots a doe a half mile off, grazing on a plateau, then another one on a hillside to the east. No bucks.

As we lay there exposed to the bitter wind at the bottom of a remote canyon, Les does something that surprises me. He hunted this canyon the day before, and sat up on this same small hill glassing in yesterday's wind. As I'm scanning the broken contours of the landscape for any twitch of an ear, checking every white spot to see if it's a mule deer's rump patch, he reaches over and hands me a three-by-three inch fragment of broken shale. On the shale he has scratched his name and yesterday's date in spidery writing. I look at it and it takes me a few seconds to realize the date is yesterday's. He sat here alone in the wind and etched his name and the date on a rock, then left it here like some memorial statement about his tiny place in the universe. I wonder for a second about what he was thinking, knowing that the odds of anyone ever seeing his scratched message were roughly zero. Yet he took the time to put his name on the rock.

In that same fleeting second I think about Norman McLean's words about his relationship with his own family at the end of *A River Runs Through It*. "Eventually, all things merge into one, and a river runs through it. The river was cut by the world's great flood and runs over rocks from the basement of time. On some of the rocks are timeless raindrops. Under the rocks are the words, and some of the words are theirs."

What is it in us that yearns for immortality, even the immortality of a few letters etched on the bottom of a piece of shale no one will ever see?

Then I think of the article I just read about an ostracon, a piece of broken pottery, that was used about three thousand years ago for a piece of scratch paper by a scribe on the border between Philistia and Judah during the reign of King Saul. That ostracon was rediscovered in an archaeological dig a few years ago and has scholars running in circles to figure out all the shapes and squiggles and what it all means. Maybe it's not so strange, this business of leaving a message for some unknown reader who may ponder it far in the future.

Of course it's less likely that an archaeologist would ever dig here, since there is so little evidence of human activity beyond a few strands of barbed wire easily explained. More likely another hunter, equally dedicated to get away from the churning mass of humanity will sit, some cold morning, on this hilltop and turn his eyes to the broken country around him, seeking game. Discouraged, he may by chance turn his eyes to the rocks, and happen to turn this particular one over, see the scratches and ponder what the letters and numbers might mean. Will he know the same alphabet? Will he use the same dating system? Or will it be totally incomprehensible to him? Who knows?

The scratches tell me far more about Les than they do about what may happen in the future. Grinning, I look up from the rock, meet his eyes, and hand it back to him. He turns it etched side down, sets it gently under the sage bush next to him, and goes back to glassing for deer.

Struggling for Life

There is an adversarial relationship between man and nature. Of course there are millions of people who will contest this. They want to see humans in a grand harmony with nature, learning to walk lightly on the earth, leaving behind only footprints. Pack out your trash and go green in every possible dimension of life, from avoiding styrofoam coffee cups to driving electric cars. I'm fully in favor of these kinds of behaviors, and I always pack out my trash and usually that of a few people who have camped or hiked or hunted before me and were not so conscientious. In the minds of these millions, any adversarial relationship between man and nature takes the form of acid rain, of carbon emissions, of global warming and industrial waste. I am troubled by these things as well. But I'm not talking about our corporate culpability for pollution of all kinds.

If you want to experience the adversarial relationship between humans and nature, just go out into it. Go out beyond the campgrounds, beyond the flush toilets, beyond the "You Are Here" maps posted by the trailhead. Get off the roads. If at all possible, go into country populated with predators. Bears. Wolves. Mountain lions. If those are too much, choose someplace with smaller hazards. Mosquitoes or scorpions will do nicely. Chiggers are good. Go at a time when the weather is being cantankerous. Twenty below zero is best. Rain will do, as will a hundred degrees in the shade.

As soon as you go out into nature on these terms, you will learn a great deal about our adversarial relationship. Hike off the trails through a swamp when the black flies are swarming. Bushwhack your way through a dense forest. Spend a night out alone in wild country without all the latest camping gear, when it's not nice weather for camping. Leave the s'mores at home. Now try to tell me that we live in basic harmony with nature.

Fact is, we will always see the disharmony, the struggle for life, when we view nature on these terms. When we see through the lens of individual experience, we will always perceive nature as a harsh taskmaster or a bitter enemy or at the very best an uncomfortable bedfellow. This is because, as soon as you enter the natural world as an individual, you become just one more organism trying to stay alive on the best terms possible, and you are de facto in competition with many other organisms out there trying to do the same thing.

This morning I walked seven miles through a peat bog in northern Minnesota. Along the way I saw tracks of moose, deer, wolves, bear, and many smaller animals. Fresh wolf tracks peppered my route. Moose trails crisscrossed the forest, and their enormous beds dotted the bog.

One year ago near this same area I encountered a lone bull moose just at dark. I was armed with a bow and arrows and had a half mile to walk to my pickup. He was in rut, drooling and calling for a cow moose, and ready to fight anything else along his trail. I spent a fairly intense twenty minutes trying to convince him that I was not a cow moose, nor did I want to fight him.

While I believe with all my heart that moose are majestic, beautiful creatures, I am wary of meeting one up close without adequate resources to protect myself. I feel the same way about wolves, though of course I know their official track record of leaving humans alone. Bears have a mixed history in encounters with humans. All the same, I go eagerly into these wild places. The fresh wolf tracks are exciting because my heart needs this experience of wilderness. In some sense I need to be reminded that my life is fragile and finite, and there are powers in the wild that will gladly take it from me.

Part of the experience is the re-entry into and the consciousness of the struggle for life. My walk this morning put me into the middle of that struggle, as I was carrying a shotgun and hoping to find ruffed grouse along my path.

What struck me as I walked, somewhere around mile four when I left the shore of the marsh where I'd been reading tracks like last night's newspaper, clambered along a beaver-dug channel and up onto the rise where poplars and ash trees grew to ruinous old age, was this: While we like to think of nature as a harmonious system, as soon as you view it from an individual level, the harmony evaporates. Along my walk, I saw a whitetail doe and fawn feeding at the edge of a fresh clearcut. As soon as they saw me, they bounded into the woods. From that doe's perspective, there is no harmony in nature. There is simply a struggle to stay alive as long and as well as possible, to find enough food and water, to reproduce, to avoid predators, including man. Yet viewed in terms of populations, you can argue that nature does an amazing job of maintaining a basic harmony. Wolf populations fluctuate in response to deer and moose numbers, and vice versa. Hard winters bring everyone down. As prey numbers rebound, wolf populations respond. It's a grand thing to watch across many square miles, over many years. But as soon as you try to keep this perspective on an individual level, you realize that life is a struggle for survival.

I heard a man talking on the radio recently about research he does with chickadees. He's discovered that in the wild, an individual chickadee finds and hides thousands of seeds during a summer. Then when the weather turns colder in the fall, that same bird will go back and eat the vast majority of those seeds. Now, chickadees don't hide their seeds in a stockpile; rather, they tuck them one at a time into the cracks in the bark of hundreds of trees.

The researcher did an experiment. He took two groups of chickadees. One he released into an environment much like the wild, where they hid seeds and when their supply ran out, they went back to try to find them. The other group he kept in an area without hiding places, but with plenty of food at all times.

After a few months, he did a neurological analysis on the two groups of birds. What he found was that the brains on the "wild" birds had thousands more active neurons than the birds who didn't have to struggle for their food or remember where they'd hidden it. Putting it simply, an easy life made the chickadees' brains lose their capability.

How often have you wished for an easy life?

For most of us, though, it seems like life is one challenge after another. We struggle to manage schedules, relationships, income and expenses. One of the things I love about hunting, about being in the wild, is that the challenges are often much clearer. I am not necessarily more successful as a hunter than I am in my "normal" life. But the thousands of daily decisions I make on the trail of a whitetail are right up there where I can see them. The struggle becomes visible.

An easy life might sound good, but it's not good for us. Not to say we don't need a break now and then to rest. Even chickadees do that. But if we take the struggle out of our lives, we end up poorer because of it.

The Kill

Last night I killed a bear.

It's been fifteen years since I went bear hunting for the first time. This is my eighth trip, near as I can count. I've had close encounters with bears, taken shots at a couple, wounded one.

Jason and I left home about 5 am yesterday morning after an intense weekend at work. Late night Sunday night, a few hours' sleep, and the five hour drive to the Shack. I had trouble keeping my eyes open the last hundred miles.

We rolled into camp and got the news from the other guys. A few promising baits, but overall pretty disappointing. We set up our stuff and claimed our bunks, got cleaned up for hunting and headed out.

I sat on the east bait. The road past the Shack snakes fifteen miles east from pavement, following a low sand ridge back into the bog. Once you get away from the highway, there are three buildings along that fifteen mile stretch: a small farmhouse on the south side of the road five miles in, a quaint hunting cabin made of logs that sits just west of the Lost River and north of the sandy road, and the Shack. Beyond the Shack the road extends not quite a mile farther. It ends in a grassy cul-de-sac.

The trail continues beyond the end of the road, into the swamp. Follow it another three fourths of a mile through the bog. Peer into the muddy pits and wonder if maybe, just maybe, the last guy who tried to cross barely escaped with his life and left his ATV down in the pit. It's not hard to imagine the tip of a handlebar protruding like a gravestone up out of the mud. Or maybe it's just a stick. Keep following where the trail climbs out of the muck and into a stand of hardwood and cedar.

Walk about seventy yards past the old bear tree. The bears used to use this massive trunk of a red pine as a marker tree when it was still alive. Since the tree died and the storm took the trunk off forty feet up, the bears don't seem to care for it anymore. Where the four little maples grow up in a cluster, leave the trail and turn left into the woods. Every twenty steps or so there's a blaze on a small pine tree or a branch broken to tell you you're on the right trail. Mostly you have to pick out the faint trail our feet have created carrying buckets of bait here.

A couple hundred yards into the trees you'll come to a clearing. I got there last night about 4 pm. The birch logs on the bait were not disturbed. I crossed the clearing and circled behind two giant cedar trees growing close together, climbed up the steps strapped around the trunk, and worked my way up to the Lone Wolf Alpha stand Les had left there. The platform hangs off the trunk, hidden behind a couple branches, a ten yard shot from the bait. You can't make mistakes sitting that close. You can't assume the bear won't see you turn your head or move your hand. You can't allow yourself to choke or cough.

For the first hour, I fought sleep. It was warm, almost hot, in spite of the fact it was the last day of September and the poplar leaves were turning gold and falling in the breeze. Sparrows happily swarmed the bait, poking around under the logs to pick at the oats left behind last time the bear licked the bait clean. A deer mouse emerged from a hole under a stump to get in on the action, but a sparrow chased it back underground. Interesting as that was, it wasn't enough. I started to drift off.

I was back at my church, working on launching this latest Alpha course. People kept talking to me about all the details. I didn't recognize any of these people, though in the dream that made perfect sense. A bearded man with a question got right up in my face and kept asking louder and louder until I woke, startled. I was still sitting upright, still fastened into my safety harness. I worried that in my sleep I might have spoken or moved, but all seemed normal, peaceful, quiet around me. The sparrows continued foraging uninterrupted.

Sleep again, then waking, over and over. Dozing on a tree stand sounds impossible for those who haven't done it, but believe me it can be done.

The last time I hunted bears was three years ago. My first night on stand during that week I am certain I had a bear coming in. I heard movement and I think I even caught a glimpse of the bear hanging out in the brush, checking out the bait. I was careless about my noise and my movement, and that week the bear shifted to only approaching the bait after dark. Nocturnal bears are terribly frustrating when you're hunting. You know they're coming to the bait, you may even have pictures on a trail camera, but you have no chance for a shot.

I was determined to keep still during this hunt. I was determined, as much as possible, to do it right. As a hunter, even if you do everything right, that's no guarantee you'll take an animal. But at least you don't have to live with the frustration of having blown your own hunt. You don't have to walk home empty-handed reliving all the ways you screwed it up. You don't have to live with the agony of inflicting meaningless pain on a wounded animal.

My legs were falling asleep, victims of a poorly padded seat. That's my only complaint about the Lone Wolf stands. I thought longingly of my Gorilla Scout, folded up in the bed of my pickup, and the thick foam padding on its seat. Switching stands would have made a lot of noise. This stand was good enough. A little physical discomfort was not beyond enduring.

After twenty minutes of dozing, physical discomfort won out over sleep. A little pain is good for the soul, right? It certainly keeps you awake. All during my time on stand, a little over an hour now, I had been hearing leaves fall through the branches. Did you know that each time a leaf strikes a branch on its wayward descent, it makes an audible noise? This noise is different from the sound when the leaf finally hits the ground. The noises of the sparrows picking oats out of the bait is quite different yet. When the breeze coming off the open expanse of the Lost River to the southwest stirs the upper leaves, it makes another noise. The poplar leaves sound different from the maples, and the cedars and firs have their own distinct sigh. There is so much to hear in the silent woods.

In the midst of this quiet cacophony I heard something else. This sound came from below me, to the northeast. It sounded like slow, heavy feet pressing down into ten inches of cedar duff. Occasionally, in the depths of the cedar mat, a small twig would break, right at the edge of hearing. A moose would probably break more branches. Unlikely a deer would come to a bait, let alone come out of the mossy swamp to my right. I was pretty sure it was a bear.

Now my motionlessness paid off. I was used to sitting still, and so I did not whirl to look. Over a period of thirty seconds, I turned my head three or four inches, just enough that out of the corner of my right eye I could see down through a gap in the branches. I was thrilled, but not surprised, when the bear crept into view.

Adrenaline does amazing things to the body. My heart rate immediately jumped to at least 150. My breath came shallow. I fought the urge to grab for my bow, to lean out for a better look. I held my teeth together. Locked my neck muscles. Relax. Relax.

Nice bear. Not big, but pretty. I was suddenly taken with awe for this animal. His long gray muzzle, small eyes, chocolate coat, his deliberate movements. He came to the base of my tree, to the very twigs I had stepped over ninety minutes earlier. He smelled, and paused. Looked back into the woods, looked back to safety.

Please come to the bait, I thought. Please come to the bait.

He sat down to think about it.

Looked up at me. Looked up the tree at me. Looked at me.

Looked back into the woods, then turned his whole body to look out into the clearing at the bait. The line of his back, the lean forward on his strong legs, the pointing of that long gray muzzle spoke of his desire for the food under those birch logs.

He circled back around, out of my sight. Then back to the bottom of my tree. What if he climbs up? I wondered. This slow, tenuous animal could clamber up my cedar for a better look at the bait, at the clearing, at me. My tiny stand would not be big enough for two of us, and I was strapped to the tree.

He looked longingly at the bait. Suddenly decisive, he took a step toward the clearing and disappeared below a couple of thick green screens of cedar. I reached for my bow. Slowly. Slowly. Don't try to lift it yet. Wait.

He got to the bait, stopped, looked back. I was right to wait. He turned to the logs, reached down with a forepaw to make a little opening, reached in for a bit of mini marshmallows and popcorn. I eased my bow off the hanger and brought it up. I was so impressed with the delicate way he ate. He took tiny bites, patient, savoring each morsel.

He stood facing directly away from me. I knew this was not a good shot. I waited. Probably only a minute, but it seemed like forever. Whatever. I was in patient mode now, waiting for the perfect shot. Time seemed to flow together. Everything was falling into place. I was in no hurry, felt no pressure. Little by little, the bear worked his way around to the right until he offered a quartering away shot. He kept his nose down in the logs, licking up the tiny morsels of food, chewing, dropping his muzzle between the logs again. Sometime during all this waiting I had clipped my release to the bowstring, just under the nock of my arrow. Slowly, slowly I pulled back until I sat at full draw.

Like a thousand times before I brought the peep sight to my eye, touched the string to the side of my nose, felt the pressure of the release along my jawline. My green sight pin centered in the circle of the peep sight over his back, over that spot I'd picked where the arrow would travel forward and down through the chest cavity. Suddenly my mind raced like lightning, running through one last check of all the details, looking for a problem, a reason to wait, and finding none. I checked the spot one last time, held the bow steady, squeezed the trigger on my release, and the arrow flew from my bow.

Everything felt right. Everything, that is, except that I was about to kill this gorgeous bear. Even that, though, was somehow right. I have spent too much time being the hunter, learning to live in harmony with taking a life, taking it well, taking it humanely. Something in my heart aches for this death. My heart both aches to avoid it, and aches to cause it and to make it count, to treasure every drop of the blood I will shed.

I read recently a story about the old Navajo hunters. The Navajo make a virtue of hozro, the sense of harmony, of living in right relationship with all other things, with circumstances, with the seasons, with the environment. They abhor death and treasure life. But the Navajo hunter must learn to be attuned differently, to find harmony with the death of another creature. So they sing the songs that bring the game to them, they sing the songs that make their arrows fly true.

For all the distance that arrow flew, it felt true. I felt the harmony of its flight, the rightness of its path. It struck home and I thought it hit well, high in the back of the ribcage where it would plunge down toward the heart.

Seeing an arrow hit the game is tricky business. I have fooled myself more times than I care to admit, thinking I had a perfect shot when later I realized the arrow was too high, or too low, or too far back. You can't go by what you see at the moment of impact.

The shot drove the bear forward, hard onto his face in the bait logs. In a millisecond he was up, whirled to his left, and ran, ran like the wind, bounded once, twice, crashed some brush off to my left. It was as if that small silent clearing exploded. As suddenly, the crashing stopped.

All this I remember only as I can force the memory to the surface, My attention was fixed on the bait pile, on my arrow, broken in two. How could this be? How could my arrow, flying straight and true toward the engrossed bear, be broken in two over the bait pile? The broadhead itself was missing, but the entire shaft of the arrow lay there in two pieces. My mind was all wrapped up in the horror of this thought: Somehow, for all my patience and preparation, for all the rightness of the moment and the release and the flight of the arrow, somehow I had messed it up. The broken arrow lay there like Exhibit A in the chain of evidence for how badly I had screwed up yet another shot. How could this be?

To my left, a dozen yards away in the brush, the bear began to cry. Hunting magazines call it a "death moan" but that doesn't begin to describe the piteous wailing that came out of the brush. It only lasted a short time. Less than a minute. But it sounded like the wailing of an unconsolable child, like a wounded toddler giving vent to a bottomless well of grief. It sounded like injustice, like life escaping, like recrimination against me.

Had the arrow hit the spine? How could that be? Maybe that would explain the broken arrow, the lost broadhead, but a spine hit would have dropped the bear right on the bait, paralyzing it for at least a moment, if not forever. A shoulder blade? I remembered what I had seen, the green and white fletching streaking toward the bear, and I could not make that shot hit a shoulder. There had been no whirl, no sudden jump at the moment of the shot. The arrow had hit, driven the bear down into the bait, and then he jumped up and ran.

The crying stopped. Not a sound from the brush behind me. No twigs snapping, no crunch of leaves. Nothing, not even a black bear, could move through that tangle quietly. He must still be there.

I checked the clock. 5:40. Two hours until dark. I promised myself I would not screw this up. The shot was done, but I would sit my backside on that stand until 6 pm. Then I would allow myself to stand up and look around. At 6:15, not before, I would climb down.

I stared down at the arrow, clean green and white vanes standing out against the leaves and dirt by the bait. No blood on the fletching. Forced myself to look away, cleared tears from my eyes. Oh, Jesus. Oh, Jesus. Oh Jesus. What happened? Followed the bear's path, saw the first set of tracks where he had torn up leaves and earth with his first bound. Blood on the leaves. A good sign, a hopeful sign. Don't think about the arrow now. I looked farther to the left, picked out his next set of tracks. Blood? Can't see.

I closed my eyes, replayed the entire sequence of events. What had I missed? Why the broken arrow? Why fourteen inches of nock, vanes, and shaft unbloodied, sitting at the point of impact? What about the rest of the shaft I could see there? What of that? My mind raced around these mysteries, finding no comfort.

Five minutes to six. I allowed myself to turn my head around and look behind me. Back in the brush I could pick out a tiny patch of black. I know from long experience that the woods are full of black patches, especially when you are thinking about bears. But this one looked blacker than the shade behind tree stumps, looked like a patch of chocolate fur in the dim light. Please God, let that be my bear. Please God, let that be my bear.

I am not in the least ashamed to say that I sat and wept on that stand. I could not give in to sobbing and hysterics, though part of me wanted to. I needed to listen. I needed not to screw this up.

5:57.

5:58.

5:59. I forced myself to look around the woods, to take inventory, to make sure a moose or another bear or a herd of pink elephants had not wandered up while I was so focused. Nothing.

6:01. Slowly, carefully, I eased my feet forward and leaned up, putting more and more weight on the balls of my feet. Finally I was standing, still harnessed into the tree, still waiting. Breathless I craned my head and shoulders around the trunk of my tree, turning to look fully behind me. There, there, there… a patch of dark fur? Please, Jesus, let that be my bear. I stood for five minutes not blinking, watching. Movement? Breath? Stirring? Nothing. Please, Jesus, let that be my bear.

Now I had to wait again, wait another eight minutes. I would not screw this up. I would not climb down before 6:15.

Finally I lowered my bow, unscrewed my bow hanger, slung my pack on my back, unhooked my safety harness, and climbed down. After nocking another broadhead, I walked first to the bait. Oh, God. Only half the arrow shaft lay there, broken. A dark branch had fooled me, looking just like the other half of the arrow. On the broken shaft, the bottom inch was bloody. The broadhead and lower shaft were nowhere to be seen. I saw no blood in the dark earth by the bait.

I walked to the tracks I had seen from the stand. Blood spattered on the leaves. Good sign. Really good sign. Oh, Jesus, let me find this bear!

Blood a little farther along, spattered like pen-and-ink witness to the speed of the bear's passage. A little more blood. So far I had moved eight yards from the bait. I looked up in the lengthening shadows, there in the dark of the cedars, and saw him. Four yards from my feet he lay motionless where I had heard him crying.

–oh Jesus oh Jesus oh Jesus–

Slowly, slowly I eased around to the front of his body. Took the arrow off my string, used the broadhead to tap him on the nose. No movement. Touched his eye with the tip of the broadhead. Nothing.

He was dead. I walked all the way around that long gray muzzle to the small patch of leaves where his front paw lay stretched out in one last attempt to run. My knees creaked a bit as I sank down in the leaves, picked up his paw, looked at the length and depth of him, felt the rough, soft pads under his feet. He was smaller than I had thought, small in a way that made him not less of a trophy but more of a beauty. "Oh, you are gorgeous!" I wept then, wept without caring. I talked to that bear, apologized for taking his life and thanked him and promised him that I would hold his life dear. "Precious in the Lord's sight is the death of his holy ones."

It was a warm evening, and I needed to take care of this kill. Gutting is never pleasant work, but it is needful. I found in the process that my arrow had indeed flown true, entering the rib cage high on the left side and exiting low on the right, just inside the right foreleg. I missed the heart by a fraction of an inch, but cut major arteries. The chest cavity was full of blood. I understood finally that I had done my part right. This bear's death had taken perhaps two minutes from the time of my shot. While that may sound like a long time, it is far more humane than any death nature could deal out to such an animal.

Now my task becomes stewardship of this bear's life. Tending the hide, rendering fat, butchering and caring for meat. This gorgeous bear has become part of me. I carry the weight of his life.

Tracking in the Dark

Jason and I were hunting whitetails at the farm where I grew up. Part of hunting deer is walking in the woods after dark or before daylight. I love doing this.

Wendell Berry wrote:

To go in the dark with a light is to know the light,
To know the dark, go dark. Go without sight,
and find that the dark, too, blooms and sings,
and is travelled by dark feet and dark wings.

Sunday night. We followed a difficult blood trail. Jason's shot came just at sunset. We started tracking after dark and spent a long time bent over, sometimes on hands and knees, examining dry leaves, looking for tiny spots of blood. We used flashlights and headlamps to try to provide enough illumination to pick out the trail, which curved and wandered, twisted and meandered. Our night vision was gone because of the flashlights. Fixed on the trail, we did not worry about directions or the easiest route back to the truck. Instead, we followed wherever the trail led.

A blood trail means you go where the animal has gone. You don't choose your route. The wounded animal chooses for you. Often this means going through the thickest brush, under low deadfalls. Wounded animals rarely follow cleared trails. So you travel light, carrying only the necessities.

There is an odd kind of submission when you're on a blood trail. Rather than choosing for myself, I follow wherever the animal chooses. I submit. As much as I might like to imagine myself a strong, independent man, in this task I relinquish my choice and follow where I am led. It's either that or abandon the trail. To choose for myself means to reject the blood trail, to let go of the bond between me and the animal whose death I have caused. Only when I submit my will to the will of the animal can I follow faithfully.

This particular trail curved back on itself, wound around in and under the trees, crossed and recrossed itself. When the blood ended we were far into the woods. We searched for a half hour, sometimes on hands and knees, sometimes bent double over the earth, but couldn't find another drop of blood or another distinctive track. We circled slowly, hoping to run across a drop or a leaf or a smudge. Painstakingly we quartered and crosshatched and stood for long moments peering into the black with our flashlight beams, trying to outguess this wounded doe.

There is a desperate kind of prayer when you lose a blood trail. You peer into the dark, down into the circle of bright light your flashlight creates, into the leaves and the dirt and the grasses and the trunks of the trees, yearning for blood, for a mark, for a broken branch that will tell you which way from here. You look up and the flashlight's afterimage is all you see for long minutes. You close your eyes and sigh and look back to the ground at your feet. You cross and recross the same ground, trying desperately to find the signs without destroying them. Nothing. Finally we marked the spot, knowing we would return again the next morning. By this time it was near midnight.

Now, how to get out? We had neglected to bring a compass. There were no direction markers, no arrows pointing to the nearest exit, no lighted walkways. Though this was not a large tract of woods, maybe a quarter by a half mile, we could easily wander in circles for hours before finding the edge of the trees, and then we might find ourselves on the far side of the forest from the truck.

We turned off our artificial lights and stood for a long time in the dark. Eventually our eyes adjusted to the blackness and we could look up through the trees. Puzzling among the branches, we finally made out Cassiopeia, Draco, and, there, Ursa Minor, with brilliant Polaris on his tail. Using the North Star as our guide, we struck a straight path to the edge of the woods, walking carefully through the tangle of brush and thorns. In a very short time we emerged into the dark alfalfa field to find the world mantled with a gorgeous wrap of open sky and bright stars. We had new wounds, cuts and scratches on hands and faces and knees. The night woods is not a gentle place.

I thought as we crossed the open field to the truck, how often we need to shut off the glare of our own lights, the shine of our own preoccupations, to trust the one who hovers above us, never changing, never lost. When we turn our eyes skyward we may find directions we had not known we needed.

And more. This business of traveling light. I have learned that there are many ways to go into the wild. Car camping is probably the easiest, where you can bring anything your heart desires that will fit into the trunk or the backseat. Want an extra jar of peanut butter? Okay, we might use that. Feel like playing Scrabble during the trip? Toss it in. Marshmallows? Yes, bring the extra bag. What about the watermelon? That will be really refreshing. Absolutely. Coolers and cots and camp chairs get thrown in or strapped on top.

Canoe camping is slightly more restrictive. You know from time to time you'll have to carry all your goods across a portage, so you whittle it down a bit. My daughter Teya and I recently spent a long weekend together in the Boundary Waters of northern Minnesota. We carefully planned our gear so that when we portaged, she carried the heavy pack, the canteens, and the paddles. I carried the lighter pack and our canoe. We were able to cross each and every portage on our route in one trip: what we affectionately call, "One-tripping it." On our final paddle back to the landing and civilization and hot showers, we met dozens of campers paddling into the Boundary Waters. One pair of canoes especially caught our attention. I'm not sure what they had in all those containers, but they were carrying more gear than I've ever seen in two canoes. It was stacked (I'm not making this up) four feet above the top of the canoes. Rubbermaid containers, packs, and cardboard boxes were all stacked like skyscrapers above the water. The canoes were loaded so heavy that they had rigged extra flotation in the form of massive styrofoam outriggers to help keep them afloat. We asked about their load as we passed, but their only explanation was, "We're planning to stay a while." We spent the next mile and a half speculating what they could have had in those containers. Most canoe campers prefer to restrict the amount of goods they carry.

Even more restrictive is backpacking. Backpackers can become obsessed with trimming an ounce here and there from their loads. They carry everything everywhere, so any amount of weight they can eliminate is a real advantage. Pat McManus, who used to write a humor column for Outdoor Life magazine, described backpackers this way:

Their gear consists of such things as silk packs, magnesium frames, dainty camp stoves. Their sleeping bags are filled with the down of unborn goose, their tents made of waterproof smoke. They carry two little packets from which they can spread out a nine-course meal. One packet contains the food and the other a freeze-dried French chef. (A Fine and Pleasant Misery)

Blood trails, however, are the lightest of all ways I know to go into the wild. You're not planning to sleep, so you don't carry a tent or sleeping bag. You're planning to track the animal, find the animal, and bring the animal out. You go as light as possible, carrying few burdens because you hope to find a burden. Only the absolute necessities for the task get stuffed in a pocket or a day bag: a knife, maybe a few granola bars and some water, a light, or maybe a couple of lights (gas lanterns seem to work really well), and orange surveyor's tape to mark the trail. An extra jacket in case it gets cold, if you happen to think of it. A length of rope for dragging the animal out.

You don't plan to stay, but I have been on blood trails that go farther into the woods than I would ever go without emergency gear. Fully grown men spend many hours grinding through the brush to drag and carry an animal out of the woods. I heard of a group of four men who drew tags for a once-in-a-lifetime moose hunt in the Boundary Waters. Far back in the wilderness, they were successful in shooting a large bull. On the way out, on average they said it took them eleven trips across each portage to get all the meat, antlers, hide, weapons, plus all their camping gear and canoes across. It was backbreaking work. I saw a picture of the group. Their grimy, exhausted smiles made them look like some of the happiest men you'd ever meet.

Traveling light is part of the blood trail because you go into the wild looking for a burden. Bill Easum, a guru who teaches successful church leaders about leadership, said a few years ago that we have operated churches for years now as though we were navigating a national park. Everything looks natural and wild, but there are maps, ranger stations, carefully placed signs, paved roads and interpretive trails. The reality, Easum said, is that the church has moved off the map into the wilderness, and wilderness navigation requires a whole different set of equipment and skills than a visit to the national park.

I've worshiped in churches that feel like a walk in the park. All of life is pre-planned joy, canned happiness, abundant Jesus-life in neat little packages like chewing gum. I wonder what happens to people in these churches when life gets messy? What happens when good parents have a son hooked on crack, or a daughter who gets an abortion? What do churches like this do when someone who is not quite ready to kick the addiction shows up in worship?

There have been times in my life when I've approached my existence, both personal and professional, like it was a backpacking trip in a national park. I've looked at maps, planned my route, made careful lists of the gear I need, figured routes and miles and pounds and campgrounds. It all looks so good in the guidebooks.

But in the times that matter, life is a lot more like a blood trail. When you get the phone call from the hospital, when you read the terse note left on the kitchen counter, when the pink slip shows up on your desk, when you're served with the papers. At such times the guidebooks go out the window. You need to start tracking, get on your knees in the middle of the night in the woods. You need to scour the leaves for spattered blood. Where is God in all this? Where has he been, and where is he going? How do I follow this trail?

Jason and I tracked that doe as long as we could that night, and came back in the morning to try again. We lost the trail, then found it, then lost it again. A couple days later my brother Les (whose land we were hunting) found the doe dead in a pond. Coyote tracks ringed the water. Les has spent almost as many hours hunting deer as I've spent breathing. He watches them, studies them, learns from them. He knows them. With that knowledge, he backtracked the doe and figured out where she'd gone, what she'd been doing. The coyotes had been ahead of us that night, pushing her on, never letting her bed down and bleed out. Their presence drove the doe beyond any reasonable behavior on that trail. The coyotes brought fear and frustration into the hunt.

Fear and frustration. Lots of times life is like that. You have an enemy that wants to mess up the blood trail, to sever the connection between you and the one who has bled for you. Fear and frustration are the trademarks of your enemy.

The good news is, Jesus is not surprised by the fear and frustration. The wildness of this trail does not intimidate him. The trail may be more than you think you can handle, but he will not leave you alone in the dark. Even when it feels like he's abandoned you, like you can't find the next drop of blood, he's there. Even when the trail doesn't take you anyplace you want to go, even in what the Bible calls "the valley of the shadow of death" he will not cut you off. It may not be a comfortable road, but his promise is that he will bring you into a good place.

Travel light. You can't afford to get weighed down with too much extra gear, or you'll never complete this trail. Don't carry so much stuff that it keeps you from following.

Pay attention. Remember that it is Jesus you're following. He has bled for you, and he has left the marks for you to follow. The trail is in the details. If you lose the trail and you are at your wits' end, wait for him. Eventually, he will provide you a way forward. You may need to shut off your flashlights, stop trusting yourself, look up and let him provide a different kind of guidance. Or you may need to keep the lights bright.

Above all, know the one you're tracking. God promises over and over in the Bible that if we seek him with all our hearts, we will truly come to know him. Move fast when you can, but not so fast you run ahead of your quarry. Don't get distracted. Keep your mind on the trail. Mark it well so others can follow.

Taking Risks

Twice in my life I have seen serious hunting injuries.

One crisp November day in the late 1980's my little brother was climbing into a tree stand when a step broke. On the way down, he dropped his rifle. It went off and sent a bullet through his right thigh. My father was hunting a quarter mile away and heard Darin calling for help. Dad had high blood pressure and was four years downstream from a brain aneurysm that had nearly killed him. That morning he ran across the plowed field to find Darin sprawled in the underbrush. Dad first tried to carry him out, but Darin was too big for that. So he wove the pickup through the trees back into the woods, and drove him home, laid out in the pickup box like a trophy buck.

I was visiting from college with a new girlfriend that weekend. Dad laid Darin out on the couch in the living room, then sat down to try to catch his breath. My girlfriend held Darin's hand while I cut off his pants leg and put into practice the first aid course I'd been taking at college that fall. We'd just studied bullet wounds the week before. Fortunately the rifle was a small caliber and the bullet missed nerves, bone, and artery. All the same, the exit wound was a jagged tear a foot long that made Darin's thigh look like it belonged on a styrofoam tray in the grocery store meat section. Three paramedics finally showed up at the door. Two of them tended Dad and one began checking Darin's leg.

When the ambulance left for the hour-long drive to the hospital, we followed in my car. Mile after mile my mind played out the scenarios of what might have been. Halfway to the hospital I pulled over to the side of the road and gave in to an all-over case of the shakes.

After surgery and some time in the hospital, Darin recovered quite well. He was playing basketball by January. Dad weathered the storm just fine.

Many years later, another treestand. Kevin (my oldest brother) and Darin struggled to fasten a tree stand onto an aging poplar as we set up for the evening bear hunt. I stood at the bottom of the tree handing up steps and helping where I could. So I had a front-row seat when Kevin started climbing down and a piece of bark tore off the tree in his hand, sending him tumbling to land on his head and one shoulder at my feet.

I was sure he was dead. I knew his neck had to be broken. He lay at a terrible angle, resting like a broken tripod on the forest floor. His knees made two legs of the tripod; the other was a messy combination of his left shoulder plowed into the pine duff, and his head pushed too far to his right side. He didn't move. Then, just as I got close and thought about how we could possibly try to move him off his twisted neck, his eyelids twitched and he threw himself backward to land flat on his back among the ferns, gasping for the breath that had been knocked from his lungs.

Darin ran a couple hundred yards out to the trail. He managed to maneuver his pickup through the trees and stumps to within forty yards of Kevin's impact, only breaking one shock mount in the process. Kevin could move all his extremities and seemed coherent. He obviously had some broken bones, and he was in a lot of pain. What to do? I still had serious misgivings about the integrity of his neck. But leaving him on the forest floor while we drove a half hour to a phone seemed unthinkable. Not to mention the hour and a half it would take an ambulance to reach us if they could even find us back in the woods. Even then we'd have to move him out to the road. So we decided to take the risk and move him. We managed to get Kevin upright, finally, and into the pickup. It was clear that both his arms, and probably some other bones, were broken. We drove back to camp and left Darin there to connect up with Les, the brother who was out on another bear bait. I took over driving. I spent a tense hour and a half trying to keep Kevin coherent. We sang a lot of old Johnny Cash songs. All the while I prayed like mad that God would tend Kevin's medical needs while I tended to driving.

An eternity later we got to the emergency room in Bemidji. The doctors took lots of x-rays and verified that Kevin's arms were broken from trying to cushion himself on the way down. The shoulder that had taken the brunt of the impact had driven downward and broke three ribs on Kevin's left side. I was quite relieved to hear that his neck and back were just fine.

Bear season lasted just a few hours that year for Kevin, but he was alive to hunt again. Many, many others have not been as fortunate.

Countless times I've been close to, or involved in, minor injuries: scrapes, cuts, falls, scratches, sprains. Hunting, by nature comes without any guarantee of safety for its participants. There's a dark humor in hunting camps. When we're sitting around a fire late at night planning the next day's hunt, if one of us is going into an especially remote area, we laugh about what it might take to find a body down that network of ravines. We speculate about which would get the corpse first after a fall: a bear or a pack of wolves?

There's an odd tension here, because the guys I hunt with are some of the most safety-conscious men I know. I've tried out a few new hunting partners and if they prove themselves careless when it comes to safety, I never go back out with them. It's not worth the risk. There is enough risk involved in these hunts that we don't need to make it worse having someone mishandle weapons, mix alcohol with shooting situations, or other simply stupid behaviors.

Yet the men I hunt with, safety-conscious as they are, recognize that hunting in remote country, taking lethal weapons high into trees and seeking out dangerous game, is a life-threatening activity. Years ago the risks seemed primarily about getting mauled by a bear or mountain lion. Lost in a snowstorm. Falling from a precipice. The last few years we've become more and more aware of the potential for heart attacks and strokes.

Two years ago I suffered a subarachnoid hemorrhage, a bleed from a broken blood vessel in my brain. It happened in early September. One helicopter ride, fifteen days in the hospital, two angiograms and two CAT scans later, the docs shook their heads and shrugged. Three weeks after I got out of the hospital, I sat down with the neurologist. I was nervous. I had been slowly, slowly re-entering my life, beginning to drive a little here and there, working a few hours, taking it very easy because that's the advice the doctors had given. This was the appointment where I would hear about the limitations, the long-term "Thou Shalt Nots" that would define my life from this point forward. I had no idea what to expect. Would my brain just explode one day? Would I live the rest of my abbreviated life waiting for the next blood vessel to pop?

Before my hemorrhage, my brothers and I had planned a Thanksgiving weekend mule deer hunt. After ten minutes of the standard non-answers from the neurologist, my head came up when he said, "I don't see any reason why you can't resume your normal life."

I looked hard at him. "No limitations?"

"No. I don't see any reason you should be limited. Do what you want."

I said, "Let me tell you 'what I want.' I want to climb up in trees and sit for hours in a stand. I want to pull a sixty-five pound bow and shoot arrows. In a couple weeks, I want to go camping in the badlands of North Dakota with my brothers. I want to sleep in a tent in freezing cold weather, on the ground. I want to carry a pack and a bow and walk ten miles a day, up and down the buttes. I want to shoot a mule deer and drag it back to camp. Are you saying I can do that?"

The neurologist looked a little stunned at my question. "Is that what you would normally do?" he finally asked.

"Every chance I get."

"Then I don't see any reason, medically speaking, you should not do it."

To my brothers' credit, once the neurologist okayed my participation they expressed no qualms. We hunted as hard that fall as we ever had, starting before daylight each morning and cooking supper in the dark. We slept in a tent in sub-zero temperatures and tried to find creative ways to keep the food in the cooler from freezing. It was a great hunt.

Wandering the coulees and buttes during those gorgeous, cold days, I thought more about the dangers inherent in hunting. I've thought about them before, usually after a close call. Just like I did on this hunt, I've always decided hunting is worth the risk. It's not quite fatalism, but there is a sense that you have to be doing something when you die, and this is a better activity than most. I'll take the risk. I'll be careful as I know how to be for the sake of those who love me, but I can't imagine giving up hunting. Besides, driving down the interstate is statistically far more dangerous, right?

The Community of Hunters

"Get that rain suit off!" My brother Les whispered barely loud enough for me to hear, but his urgency came out in a tight motion of his hand, low, by his knee, so the movement would be hidden by the poplar tree where he crouched. I realized it was not worth staying dry if the noise of my rain gear blew the hunt. Darin was a few yards ahead offering up a creditable imitation of a bull elk bugling. For a week now the three of us had been in the White River country of Colorado, hunting at about ten thousand feet. We had each seen elk from a distance. Half a mile, a mile away across a canyon or far up in a mountain meadow, we watched them graze. We'd hunted in the sun, in the heat, in the dry, thin air of Colorado in September. We'd put more miles on our feet and our four-wheelers than we could count, but we'd failed to get close to an elk.

This morning the plan was different. Instead of hunting alone as we had done all week, we'd go together out on one long ridge. We'd seen good sign there. Les thought there might be elk near one particular waterhole along the crest. It was the last day of a week long hunt. We dreaded packing our gear and driving back to Minnesota empty handed.

The weather changed overnight. In a matter of a few hours, high country heat gave way to drizzle and cool air. A good omen. The elk would be more active in the cooler temperatures. Rain would be uncomfortable for us, but what is a hunt without some discomfort? Altitude sickness and sore muscles were obviously not enough; we ventured out into the dark, into the cold morning mist. Just to get to the ridge we planned to hunt we'd have to ride through a morning chill that froze our fingers to the handlebars of the four wheelers. For the first time this week the words "wind chill" crossed our minds. Then we'd hike down a dark slope overrun three years earlier by forest fire, now full of dog-hair alder and the burned out, tangled trunks of logs. Just climbing up and down the slope felt like a full day in football training camp. Then we'd ascend the far side, where rain made the clay slick and nearly impossible to navigate standing up. We'd try to do all this silently in hopes that a bull would be hanging around the spring at the top of the ridge.

We'd worked our way out on the crest of the ridge, and our hearts raced to hear bulls bugling down the far slope a couple miles away. We abandoned the spring and hustled through the brush to the south, toward the elk. Darin bugled once, and a bull answered. We moved a couple hundred yards through the wet brush. Darin bugled again. The answer this time was closer, and then another answer came from a different direction. We had at least two bulls responding.

It was at that moment Les noticed how much noise my rain gear was making. I quickly shucked out of my pants and jacket and stuffed them wet into my daypack. The bulls were still half a mile down the ridge, so we crept south again.

It was a dream hunt. Les had been to Colorado after elk once before, but neither Darin nor I had ever hunted elk before. We'd had a blast camping together, as we always do. We hunt serious on these trips, worrying more about hours in the field and finding game than about food, sleep, entertainment, or comfort. Each night we'd return to camp late, cook something solid for supper under the stars and fall into our sleeping bags. We rose before dawn the next morning to do it all again on a granola bar for breakfast and a sandwich tucked in a pocket for lunch.

The bulls had fallen silent. Where were they? We crept on. Les emerged from the big trees into a clearcut. A pile of old slash hung on the brow of the ridge where it dropped off to the west, and he circled up behind it, using the pile for cover. Darin walked twenty yards behind Les and took the near corner of the brush pile. Darin's next bugle caught me in the open, another ten yards behind Darin in waist-high fireweed next to a couple stubby tree stumps leftover from a logging expedition some years before. When he let out that eerie call, the answer came immediately, from less than a hundred yards down the ridge. The hair stood up on the back of our necks and we dropped where we stood. Arrows went on strings. We crouched peering into the brush, all ears, hoping for more. Just as our heartbeats began to slow, the bull appeared, antlers rising first over the brush pile like the periscope of a submarine surfacing. Six hundred pounds of bull elk trotted out of nowhere and strode up to the edge of the clearcut. Head up, nostrils flared, he looked around, seeking the bull that had challenged him moments before.

He saw me. From twelve yards away, he locked eyes with me. I was exposed, crouched in the weeds, trying with all my might to look like a tree stump. He didn't buy it. I'm a little superstitious about how wild animals sense things, so I broke eye contact. I shifted my gaze to his ribcage, to the matted hair just behind his foreleg, the spot where I'd put an arrow if I could. I thought as calmly as I could, "Look away. Just look away. Look back down the ridge behind you." Who knows if such suggestions do any good in a crunch?

My wishing didn't seem to influence the bull. He knew I didn't belong, and he was determined to figure me out. My heart hammered my ribs and I worried that the little panting noises I could hear in my throat, the sound of blood rushing through my carotid arteries, would spook the bull. I held still, arrow ready, my release on the string, prepared at any second to raise my bow four inches higher and draw if he would just look away. He stared at me.

In that second, that eternal second, I heard Darin's release and the thwup! as his arrow took the bull in the chest. From his vantage point he'd been able to see the bull earlier than I had. He drew his arrow while the bull came up behind the brush pile. After waiting for me to shoot, Darin realized the bull had me pinned and took the shot himself.

The elk whirled away and crashed down the slope. We listened until the sound of breaking brush stopped a few seconds later. At that moment a little raghorn bull came up from the south, and a cow appeared just to the east of us. A third small bull came through a few minutes later. In fifteen minutes, we had four different elk on three sides of us, less than fifty yards away. Then, like early morning dreams, they vanished.

We checked our watches and forced ourselves to wait a few minutes more. Huddled together, we whispered excitedly about the incredible experience we'd just had. A few moments had been captured on the video camera Darin carried, but no footage of the bigger bull he'd shot.

Then it was time. We went looking for the blood trail. Les found clear sign twenty yards down the slope. We followed over deadfalls and through patches of fireweed. It was not a difficult trail. Sixty yards from the top of the ridge we found the bull sprawled on the slope. Darin's arrow had pierced his heart and one lung.

We paused for a few awe-struck, giddy pictures. We marveled at the beauty of the bull. We rehearsed over and over again how it had all happened. We talked like madmen, mad with joy, ecstatic about this unbelievable day, about the fact that we were all together, that this was a hunt we truly shared. We memorized the sequence of the elk coming in and compared notes on what each of us saw, what each of us experienced. It was only then Darin learned that I hadn't had a chance to draw. Only then did I learn Darin had seen the bull three or four seconds before he emerged right in front of me, so he'd had a chance to pull his arrow back. Darin and I had seen only one of the younger bulls, so Les delighted to fill us in.

Delight finally gave way to duty. The three of us together were barely enough to turn the bull around so his head lay uphill to make gutting easier. Once that chore was done we paused to divide our labor. How best to get the meat, cape, and antlers back to camp?

In addition to farming, Les owns a taxidermy business. He knows well how to roll an animal out of its skin and how to take the meat off the bones. We agreed he would stay and butcher the elk while Darin and I made the long trek back across the ridge, down the slippery trail, and up the burned-over slope to the four wheelers. We could drive four miles around and come in from the northwest. That would allow us to get within about a quarter mile of the elk and avoid the up-and-down of the ridge.

When we returned after an hour and a half, Les had the bull nearly butchered. We began to layer meat in our packs and haul load after load up the valley to our parking spot. My pack was full first, and all eager I started out ahead of the others. We'd been packing the meat in garbage bags to keep it free from dirt and flies, so at the four wheelers I stashed the heavy, blood-wet garbage bags and turned with my empty, blood-soaked pack back toward the elk. Five minutes later I met Les and Darin loaded down on their first trip out.

On the way back, I somehow missed the elk. The side of the ridge was a couple hundred yards from bottom to top, and one clump of pines looks much like another. I must have gone too low on the slope, back there where the trails diverged. How far down the ridge had I gone? I slowed to think, to compare landmarks. When I was certain I'd gone too far south and missed our spot, I turned around. Just at that moment I noticed bear droppings, fresh, in the muddy trail. Clear paw prints let me know that this bear was a recent visitor. I thought of the meat still at the kill site, and then I thought of the blood-soaked pack on my back. I turned and began to walk back north, angling up the ridge, with new determination.

After a few minutes I heard Darin call my name, at least three hundred yards north up the ridge. He'd logged the kill in his GPS as a waypoint, so he had no trouble finding it. When he and Les returned and didn't find me there, he shouted. I came back and told them about the bear sign. We loaded our packs heavy and made another trip, all together this time. A third trip with the last of the meat, the antlers, and the cape and we were done.

I thought as we left the site for the last time about the way a Ute hunting party or a pair of mountain men might have handled things a century or two before. They would have brought the entire family and camped by the kill, no doubt, cooking up some of the parts we left behind: the meaty ribs, the tongue, the heart. They might well have built fires right there and made A-frame racks, cutting meat into strips and jerking it over the smoky flames. Bones and sinew would have been harvested, dried, fashioned and stored for later use. I felt a pang of guilt, thinking of the example of these hunters who were so much more thorough than we were. The sad truth is that they had days and weeks to spend on a kill, and we had to leave the plateau the following day to drive twelve hours home on the interstate.

That night, back in camp, we filled the coolers full of fresh meat, packed up our gear, loaded the four wheelers on the trailer, tucked the antlers in on top and strapped everything down. Tired to the bone, we cooked elk backstraps over an open fire, washed it down with the last few lukewarm beers in camp and rolled into bed happy men. We woke to a landscape newly covered with snow the next morning, packed the soggy tent in with the rest of the gear, and started for home.

I tell this story in such detail because it brings me vividly back into the camaraderie, the community, of that hunt. There is nothing like the fellowship of hunters. I believe that if we could somehow reach across time and touch the minds of that Ute hunting party or men like Jedidiah Smith or Jim Bowie, we would find a kinship, an understanding, based on our common identity as hunters. These are men who knew the joy and the heartbreak of a fresh kill, who understood that life and death walk in the same footprints, who could have sat around that fire eating fresh elk and been as content as we were.

When I read the gospels, I see a similar kind of fellowship among Jesus and his disciples. They didn't always understand it, but there was something in following Jesus that drew burly men like Peter and Andrew, James and John, to walk away from other pursuits. When Jesus was finally driven to explain what it meant to follow him, his words sound a lot like they come from a blood trail or an elk kill, only Jesus talks about his own death. "Unless you eat my flesh and drink my blood," Jesus tells them, "you have no life in you" (see John 6:53 and following).

Those who heard his words struggled to make sense of them, much like I have struggled to make sense of my love of the wilderness, or much as I have struggled to make sense of how I am to follow Jesus. Many of them were not up to the task. "This is a hard word," they said, "who can accept it?" When Jesus didn't make things any easier for them, they grumbled and walked away to find a different rabbi, a different trail to follow.

Jesus turned to his closest followers. "Are you leaving too?" he asked.

Peter spoke up for the group, and I think his words have the ring of late night campfires and long talks about the meaning of it all. He talks like a man who has sat in silence hour after hour, day after day, wrestling and pondering and wondering. He talks like one who recognizes truth when he bites into it. "Lord, to whom shall we go? You have the words of eternal life." There was something about Jesus, something in his words and his actions and his hands and his eyes, something in his life, that had Peter and the others by the throat. They couldn't leave now. They were bound together in a fellowship of life and death.

Soon it would become a fellowship of blood, when they fled in fear from the garden of Gethsemane, when they saw Jesus flogged, his blood running on the paving stones, and then crucified; when they watched him impaled on a Roman spear, bleeding out on the hillside west of Jerusalem. They were united by the blood trail of Jesus, by his words and the long habit of following him, by the conviction that he was indeed the way, and the truth, and the life. Easter morning was a terrible, wonderful shock to their systems. Meeting Jesus alive again after that horrendous Friday took them years to unravel. But that experience of his resurrection hooked them permanently into his trail. They belonged totally to him now, and to each other. Each of those men, and many others, would give their lives for this following. They would die, some sooner, some later, bound by blood and new life to Jesus and to one another.

You want to be careful who you invite onto a blood trail with you. A good partner can make the hunt; a poor one can break it. Several years ago I had a difficult trail to follow, trying to find a poorly hit doe. I'd left her overnight, and a dusting of snow had covered the trail. In sheltered places you could still see the dark spots where the blood had dropped; in open areas enough snow accumulated to cover the trail. Sometimes I followed just her footprints, tracing them in and out of other tracks, other trails, following cautiously enough to find blood again when we passed through heavier brush.

An eager companion came along on that trail, all excited to help me find the doe. He was an older man so I deferred to him out of respect. However, in his excitement and inexperience he bounded ahead, stepping in the deep snow right on top of her tracks before I noticed or could say anything. I looked up from examining a few drops of crimson on the snow, trying to determine where the doe was hit by examining the blood, to find that he had destroyed the trail. We couldn't find the doe's trail again. Needless to say, I won't bring him along on another hunt without clear boundaries.

Who follows the blood trail with you? I've learned to judge hunting companions not so much by whether they can make the shot, but by what happens after. We are united in a sacred pursuit. Respect for the animal means nothing less. The community of hunters, bound together by blood, is too precious.

Over the last decade I have worked hard to cultivate a place in a community of men. It is painstaking work. It is worth every ounce of effort I have poured into it. Today I have a few close friends who, when necessary, will hold my torn heart precious. They have done so. I have returned the favor, sitting with them in the crisis, in the grief, in the face of the hard questions.

It takes time and intentional effort to build this kind of trust, this kind of brotherhood. Some of us have hunted together, canoed together, camped together, worked together, played together, prayed together. This community is not a club. There's no membership, no dues, no roll call. These are simply the guys I call, or who call me, when we're on a blood trail.

Winter

Winter Hunt

It's dark yet, though the sky is gray, not black, out east. Orion marches across the sky, but he's fading. Snow is dry and powdery, thank goodness. Deer will move like ghosts in this stuff. Little bit of fog coming up. That will get worse before it gets better, I think.

Edge of the woods, though the trail is wide through here. Gene used to bring his tractor through here in the winter cutting wood and it packed the dirt so thorns and underbrush don't take over so much on this pathway. Something did, anyway; this trail has been wide and open as long as I remember. It follows right along the line where the poplars give way to oak, just on the edge of the rise.

When I was a child this patch of woods was off limits. Gene didn't like trespassers, family or no. We stayed out, mostly, except for the time we snuck in to raid the apple trees on the south end of the woods. He walked in on us, buckets half full of those sweet crab apples. Gene was not happy. He confiscated our harvest and sent us off empty-handed with a few memorable words.

So these woods remained a mystery for many years. Imagination could run wild, looking across the open field where we used to pasture the heifers to the dark tree line where the oaks took over, one strand of electrified wire hung to keep the heifers from wandering into "here-there-be-dragons" forever.

Gene's been gone thirty years now, I guess. Fence came down and that pasture was cut up to be a wheat field. Soybeans now, more money. Deer love the stubble sticking up through the snow, a few pods here and there in the dry wind.

Dark enough under the trees I have to use a headlamp. I could wait ten minutes. Light is coming fast now. But I don't want to be walking after daybreak. So I do my best to slide through the trees like the deer do, like ghosts in a fog, like submarines easing along the bottom of some white ocean full of giant, woody seaweed. No way a human can move that quiet. But I try. I'm headed for the stand along the little round grassy swamp, a stand at the heart of these trees. The deer will be coming back to bed there in an hour, making their slow, cautious way through the brightening woods, eager to take refuge from the daylight. I'll be waiting.

I've been walking just a hair faster, downhill. Just as the land begins to rise under my boots, I see the four trees together, planks pegged into them, seat cobbled onto one side of the platform. Careful now. Hoarfrost on the steps. Slow and quiet, for all the good it does. Fourteen feet up in the trees I settle on the platform and it goes off like a rifle shot in the almost dark. Lumber squeaks like a strangled squirrel at this temperature, and I try to lower my weight without alerting the whole county. Within seconds the stand has adjusted to my presence and I vow I won't even take a deep breath for fear of this stand making those awful noises again.

So I sit quiet. Lots to think about as the daylight creeps over the world. Fog is spreading like I figured. Something about woods in fog. Easy to get lost; all the edges go soft and navigation is tough. But there's a gentleness to the woods when the clouds rest on the ground, too. Absolutely quiet. Nothing flying, nothing talking yet. In a few minutes the red squirrels off to the southwest will be awake and moving and making plenty of noise, but for now silence holds this wood like a vise. Twenty degrees warmer, or thirty, maybe, and the fog would be dripping off the branches. But as it is, the only sound is crystals of frost forming on the upper branches, too faint for me to hear. I bet if I could hear that it would sound like angels singing. In an hour, maybe, it will be worth taking a picture of this woods from out by the road. All these trees will look like a fairyland. Right now you'd just see fog in the gray pre-dawn.

Little by little, so slowly you don't notice, while you're thinking about other things, it gets light. You look around and realize there's nothing you can't see now. It's so different from hunting at nightfall. At night you sit and wait and hope and every minute that goes past makes it more and more likely that the deer will show up, right at dark, and your adrenaline courses just to think about it, until finally there comes that moment when you face reality, you admit that you can no longer tell the colors of your sight pins, you can no longer pick them out against the dark trunks of the oaks, and it's time to leave. In the mornings, though, everything happens much slower. The light comes when you don't expect it, and you never know if the deer are coming or not, and if they do one moment is as good as the next. Adrenaline is hard to come by, and it's cold.

The fog helps. It feels colder. There's no way on earth to stay warm; no parka can shut out the frigid humidity of a winter fog. But the fog helps because it gives your mind something to do other than worry about the cold. You try to pick out shapes, try to see movement. It's not just looking around at the trees, it's peering, it's trying to pierce the fog with your eyes, trying to light a fire with your eyes that will burn away this gray softness that rests on the world so that you feel like someone trying to breathe under icy sheets, frozen quilted covers in a too-big bed. You squint at the shapes in the fog and you convince yourself that this one, then that one, is moving. Then, out of the corner of your eye you do see the line of a back, then ahead of it an ear, and you realize that seventy, eighty yards away there is a deer walking through the woods but it is gone now and you have to tell yourself it's okay to exhale, but slow, so that you don't whistle, because it might come back this way. If one is moving, the others are probably coming as well. After a few minutes your eyes ache from trying to see the others but there are no others, it's a solitary animal, which sends you into another dizzy spiral of thought: was it a buck?

There's been nothing for twenty minutes now. I don't think I ever saw that deer, I imagined it. I was starting to doze off. Fog's starting to burn off now. Edges are starting to firm up, the trees are getting hard again, everything is becoming crisp except the little branches that have become a wonderland of Jack Frost artistry, wondrous sculptures in tiny ice crystals that will feel miserable down the back of your neck on the walk out.

The red squirrels have had their say now and moved back to their trees until the sun gets higher. Chickadees came through for a few minutes too, but they need to keep moving. One perched for a second right there, right on that branch just ten inches from the tip of my nose, checking me out, I guess. Thought he might try the brim of my hat, but he didn't.

Something about morning in winter in the woods. Like you're Adam in the garden, only God forgot to turn off the ice age. If it wasn't such a cliche, I'd say it felt holy. Or maybe whole. Life in all its glorious wonder, there in the body of that one little chickadee, the only wildlife you've seen for sure all morning. How can that body no bigger than a marshmallow live in this deep freeze? Where do they go when it gets really cold? Those tiny, vulnerable, exposed feet, and what can you eat in these woods that will keep you going, little bird? The surfaces of things in the winter seem sterile, like you could do surgery on them. Nothing lives here. But the little birds do, and their confident mumbling doesn't sound desperate or fearful at all. They talk like they're grocery shopping.

Climbing down is hard, since my joints have stiffened up. I think if I fall I'll shatter. I can feel the cold like an icy leech wrapped around my ribs and my neck, sucking the heat out of me. Finally I'm down, and safe in the snow again I start to pick my way back up my footprints. Not fifty yards up the trail I cross

a set of deer tracks, fresh, over my own prints. Well. Stopped
there and looked at me, I just bet. I had no idea. Just kept on
going on his way.

I feel like the woods, deep down below consciousness, is
watching. Waiting for me to leave. Eager for my disturbance to
be over, eager to go back to the cold hard patience of winter. So I
keep moving, hoping if I do my hands will thaw, looking forward
to a cup of coffee in a warm kitchen.

I wouldn't trade this morning for anything.

What time is it?

Timing is everything when you're hunting. Hunting whitetails, for example, it's important to know what time it is. Hunting for whitetails in mid-September is a whole different ball game than late November. Timing your hunt means you know what they're eating, where they're moving, what's on their minds when you want to hunt. Hunting magazines publish article after article about timing. They write about acorns, alfalfa, hazelnuts, and other food sources. They write more than anything about the rut and how to hunt pre-rut, early rut, late rut, after the rut. It's possible to just go sit in the woods and get lucky, but your odds go up considerably if you know the deer and understand their timing.

Even the act of taking a shot requires careful timing. Last winter I was on stand on the very last evening of bow season, which in Minnesota is December 31st. Over the years I have come to care less about the end of the calendar year than I do about the end of bowhunting season. Too often I end the year thinking about an unfilled tag. Though I tried that afternoon to ignore the clock, to remain in the moment, in the back of my brain the minutes ticked away. Two hours to the end of the season. Ninety minutes. One hour. Thirty minutes. As the sun plunged toward the horizon, then began to disappear behind the trees to the west, I started to grieve another season of great hunting mixed with great disappointment. I had seen deer from this stand all fall: seventy-five yards, sixty yards, a hundred yards. I longed for one opportunity to shoot, and slowly I turned my heart toward the old familiar disappointment. I took some small consolation in the old saying that experience is what you get when you didn't get what you want.

Then the doe appeared. She crossed the gap to my left and sniffed my decoy. She wandered into the trees on the trail past my stand. When her eyes went behind the big oak, I drew back to shoot. Motion made my stand creak in the bone-numbing cold and she jumped off the trail, back into the brush. I stood at full draw, waiting. Waiting. Ten seconds. Twenty. Thirty. My arms strained with the tension. As she stood, head high and alert, I focused on a spot behind her shoulder. She stepped once, twice, paused, stepped again, stepped into the opening. I released. The arrow flew home just as the sun disappeared below the horizon on the last day of the season. Timing.

Time is also a delicate thing on a blood trail. After the shot, you have to give the animal time to die. Contrary to the movies, death from gunshot or arrow is not instantaneous, not even with a perfect hit. It takes at least a few minutes. After a shot, I try to remember immediately to check the clock. This is less about knowing when I made the shot and more about forcing myself to wait thirty minutes before I start down the trail. In that heart-pounding moment, if I trusted my instincts, I would follow hard on the heels of the wounded animal after an excruciating wait of three or four minutes that would seem like eternity. Even with a perfect shot, a half hour is critical. After a poor shot, I'll wait hours, even overnight, before starting down the trail. Good hunters can tell you that those sleepless nights after a poor shot are horrible. You replay the shot and all the factors that went into it. You relive that twitch of your release, the way you dropped your bow arm, the gust of wind or the animal turning the wrong way at the last second. You see it over and over during the night, experiencing over and over again a tiny mistake that has led to drastic consequences. You hope against hope that come daylight, the trail will be good and you'll recover the animal.

Let's say for the moment the shot is good. Those thirty minutes you wait may mean that the animal has time to bed down and quietly bleed out. Usually the animal is dead long before a half hour is up, but an impatient tracker and a less-than-perfect hit means the animal jumps and runs and may not stop for a long time. A half hour can mean the difference between losing and finding, between success and failure, between meat and hunger.

During that half hour wait, you replay the shot. As a hunter grows more experienced, one of the things that changes is he (or she) becomes much more realistic in assessing the shot. Was it the center of the chest, double-lung pass through shot you hope for? Or did you hit the shoulder blade? What was the sound of the impact when the arrow hit home? How did the animal react? An animal that stood, startled and alert, after the shot is probably hit well. If the animal hunches its back, though, you're likely dealing with a shot that is too far back, in the liver or the stomach. Knowing the difference, knowing what to look for, helps you discern the correct timing for the trail.

Other factors, though, may force the tracker to move quicker. If snow or rain is falling, a half hour's wait may mean the trail washes away or gets buried. It's not enough to know the animal; you also have to know the weather. A blood trail can be a delicate balance between waiting and pushing forward, between patience and assertiveness.

So much of life depends on timing. I'm constantly trying to assess the timing of what God is doing in my life. I try to read his tracks, to watch his actions, to pay attention to what he is doing. Often his timing requires more patience, more waiting, than I would choose. But just like in hunting, patience often pays off.

My older daughter is in her third year of college. We had the strategy meeting the other night. How many classes do you have left? When can you fit them into your schedule? How many semesters will this take? What are your plans? Where is God calling you? What do you want to be when you grow up? To my credit, I did not ask the question that too often dominates my thoughts about her schooling: How many more semesters will you be wanting me to pay for your education? I try not to push too hard with these things, but we needed to touch base. So I asked the where-is-God-at-work-in-your- education questions and tried hard to listen to her responses, to hear where God has been moving in her life, to discern what he's doing. To pay attention to the timing, to read the tracks. She is an incredibly smart and talented young woman, and I have always been confident God has great things planned for her. But he doesn't unfold those plans on my schedule.

As we talked, she came to a moment that I have to describe as a revelation. Suddenly, in one intense two-minute burst, she articulated what she wants to do, where God is leading her heart, how she wants to spend her life. It was amazing for me to be there, to have a front row seat, to watch it happen. At one point, eyes bright, she blurted, "I can see now, I can see how everything in my life–everything–points me this direction. And there's no way I could have known it before now. If I had known, it would have ruined the whole thing." She recited a long list of some of the most difficult things she's been through in her life, going back many years in some cases, and she pointed out how each of those experiences shaped her, directed her, prepared her for this calling.

Looking back on that conversation, seeing God's call for her unfolding, I am amazed at his timing. His plans unfolded at exactly the right time, not too early, not too late. This is not a done deal, of course. This road will have many twists and turns before she is done. But right now, she has amazing clarity and perspective and determination and excitement. It's a good time.

Most of the frustration in my life has to do with timing. I know that God has good plans for me, too, but I don't see them unfolding as I choose. Seems like I spend a lot of time blundering about in the dark, feeling for the light switch. The last few months I've been enduring a wrestling match with burnout. It's been one of those periodic times of frustration and dissatisfaction I hit about every two years. I've been through mild cases of burnout before, but this one has been rough.

In the middle of this burnout, I've been reading a book on the recommendation of a coworker. It's called *Stuck!* and it deals with times of transition. Terry Walling, the author, describes what happens during these difficult, frustrating times, and then he goes a step further to ask, "What is God doing during this time?" Other times in my life I would have thought the book was so-so, but right now I've been devouring it. The timing is perfect.

I wonder about God's sense of timing. A few different places in the Bible we read that for God a thousand years could just as well be a day, or a day a thousand years. You might have heard the old joke about the man who asked God, "What is a thousand years to you?"

God answered, "It's like a minute."

Then the man asked, "What is a million dollars to you?"

God answered, "It's like a penny."

The man thought for a moment, then asked, "Can I have a penny?"

God answered, "In a minute."

What does timing look like to God? I doubt the hours and days look the same to him as they do to me. I see the slow parade of seconds, one after the other like boxcars rolling past an intersection as I sit in neutral and the red lights blink. I wonder if he sees instead the intersections, the places in time where opportunities come together, where the conversation or the revelation happens, the on-ramps and off-ramps of my life where he places opportunity in my path. I wonder if he sees the preparation and the potential instead of the ticking of the clock. I wonder if from God's perspective, the wearing down of my stubbornness, the all-too-slow opening of my eyes, is the important part of timing. He's like a hunter, waiting motionless and silent for me to emerge from the brush, waiting for the perfect opportunity, waiting to make the shot that will slay my stubborn heart, that will bring me to the point of surrender.

New Year's Eve again. I could see from my stand that the blood trail was obvious on the snow. Checking the clock, I finally climbed down, marked the spot where she stood when I released, and began to follow the trail. She had run at breakneck speed far into the dim light under the trees, and I followed her trail, good blood all the way, for a hundred yards or a little more. She lay in the snow on the hillside, stretched on the uphill side of the trail as if she'd just run out of momentum and fallen the way a tree slowly topples. As the light of the old year ran out, I cared for her body, my hands and forearms red and bloody, a silly grin spattered across my face. I carefully loaded her on a sled and brought her back across the snow, sliding step by step through the dark.

All that night the human world around me watched the ball drop in Times Square. People marked the boxcar-like passage of another year. They resolved to lose weight, quit drinking, eat better, or start going to the gym. Giddy people partied and toasted and sang and kissed and laughed.

I worked in the quiet dark and marveled at the timing of a good hunt. What a way to spend time. What a way to close out a season. What a way to end a year, and to begin anew.

Spring

Ellingson's Swamp

"Which way to the road?" My stubby seven-year-old legs had been following Dad through an unfamiliar (to me) patch of woods we called Ellingson's Swamp. We had worked our way through the brush a couple hundred yards to the edge of a large pond. Standing by the shore, we watched beavers gliding through the water leaving a giant "V" behind them. Their tiny wakes spread across the whole pond, waves lapping at the edge by our feet. Dad whispered that sometimes he had seen moose here. They seemed to like the pond, he said.

"Does anything else live here?" I asked.

He talked of foxes, deer, and crows. I marveled in wonder at the spectacle of the pond, the beavers, and the unseen presence of moose and so many other creatures. This swamp was an amazing wilderness and it was less than a mile from my front door.

Time to go. He asked me, "Which way to the road?" He pretended not to know, though I knew better. I had no fear, no sense that anything could invade this place at this time that might overwhelm my father. He was the picture of strength, knowledge, and competence. In these woods, he was a man in his element.

I looked at the sky, looked around at the trees, looked out at the water, and pointed in what I hoped was the right direction. "That way."

Dad laughed. He said, "We could go that way, but it might take us a while to get back to the road. How about we try this way?" He then led me in almost the opposite direction to the one I had chosen. A few steps for his long legs, it seemed, and we emerged on the road.

I learned about hunting and about life and about manhood in a thousand encounters like this one. Sometimes, though less often than I would have liked, my father led me into the woods. More often I was the tagalong to my two older brothers, scrambling desperately to stay on their heels. I did all I could to soak in the knowledge they imparted, and to endure their sometimes severe teaching methods. In fairness, they were mostly tolerant teachers and they took good care of me. The two of them used to imagine that they were Meriweather Lewis and William Clark on their great expedition. They debated a bit about who I could be. They finally decided that it couldn't be just the Lewis & Clark Expedition if I was along. It must be Lewis & Clark & then some. They pointed at me and said, "You're Thensome."

Growing up, my home nestled in the middle of wide rural lands. A mix of deciduous woods and farmlands surrounded us for miles. The farms of neighbors butted up against our own. In those days, and at that age, property lines seemed less important. We wandered freely, hunting and exploring where we liked.

Frequently, especially as I grew older, I learned about the wilderness near my home by venturing out into it alone. Sometimes these were hunts for rabbits or grouse, sometimes just expeditions for the sake of finding new trees, new haunts, or visiting favorite spots. I tried once every year or two to make sure I visited the waterfall in Harstad's woods. When I felt especially daring I would trespass to find out if Gene's apple trees were bearing fruit. I'd sit on the edge of the pit that marked the site of the old root cellar southeast of Grandma Pederson's house and ponder my ancestors who had stored food here for winter. There were also a hundred other spots that didn't have names. These places were the schoolroom where I learned to handle myself, where I learned to hunt. All these places were within two or three miles of my home and I could walk there and back again.

Then, on a whole different level, there was the Shack. My father and his buddies had started hunting the Pine Island State Forest north of Bemidji back in the 1950's, and eventually they signed a lease agreement with the state to put an old tar paper shack fifteen miles back on the Lost River Road. Our family didn't go on vacations per se; instead, a couple times a year we went up to the Shack. Picnic baskets, coffee thermoses, sleeping bags, an outboard motor and binoculars went in the back of the pickup or sometimes in the back of the station wagon. We loaded up the family, and we went to play. The Shack stands on a low sand ridge that stretches miles from the nearest paved road, rising a couple feet over the surrounding peat bog. There is just enough elevation to allow a decent roadbed. On this sandy track, logging trucks and pickups full of grouse hunters pass deep into the boggy woods of northern Minnesota. Moose, bears, wolves, deer, chipmunks and skunks fill those woods. The sandy road provides a great chalkboard for reading tracks.

If the woods around my home made up my elementary school classroom in regards to hunting, the area around the Shack was high school and eventually college. We picked blueberries and listened for wolf howls, and Dad told stories of hunting expeditions with his gang. We learned the geography and the names that rang with mystery and challenge: the Old Buck Trail, the Buck Island Trail, the Lost River and the Little Tamarack. Summers we would drive the twenty miles from the Shack out to the tiny burg of Waskish, rent a twelve foot aluminum Lund boat, bolt the old seven and a half horse Johnson motor onto it, and venture out the mouth of the Tamarack into the wide waters of Upper Red Lake. This shallow lake was so broad it was hard to see the opposite shore. My mental image of Jesus and his disciples on the Sea of Galilee has been forever shaped by those walleye fishing expeditions out among the rolling waves.

Back in the woods, Dad taught us to prime the old iron pump that brought "running water" into the Shack. We learned to drive slowly (never more than twenty miles an hour) down the sandy roads, anticipating at any moment a deer bounding across the road or, more often, an interesting set of tracks in the sand. He taught us to walk silently down the trails, and to always be noticing and considering what the wildlife around us might be doing. He taught us to pay attention.

All these reminiscences lead me to a point. Namely, hunting is a gift given to the next generation. This may mean that children learn from their parents, as I did. I have tried intentionally to draw my daughters into a fascination with the natural world, into the experience of hunting, into an awareness of lives other than theirs, and what their life may cost. This has nothing to do with whether they choose as adults to take up bow or gun and hunt, though I often hope they will. They have the freedom to choose that or not. But as their father, I have done my best to give them the lessons that only intimacy with the natural world in all its brutish violence and stunning beauty can provide.

In these days when the number of hunters has declined dramatically, hunting is often a gift given from one friend to another. I've had the privilege of introducing several friends to hunting. Jason asked a few years ago if I'd take him hunting. We went, of course, to the Shack. In spite of a weekend of driving rain and a distinct lack of grouse, he was hooked. We have hunted together many times since, and I've had the privilege of taking him to many of the places that are etched on my soul. We were back on the farm where I grew up, walking together near Gene's apple trees when he spooked a whitetail doe along the edge of the field, and I made a running shot that filled my tag that year. He arrowed his first black bear a few miles from the Shack.

It is an honor to bring a person who has never hunted into the woods. Of course, some "get it" and others don't. I'm always amazed to watch the ones that get it. There is a growth, a maturing, a depth that comes from contact with wild things. Something primal in us rises up to greet and grow into the practice of hunting, of sleeping outdoors, of hours on stand, of walking a dark trail back to camp at the end of a long day's hunt. Men especially seem to be always seeking to prove themselves, and the hunt is in our genes. This is the proving ground that matters. Those that have met this challenge grow into themselves in a way that screen-based reality can never provide.

Here is the sad truth of video games and most other entertainments: They cost you nothing, and they gain you nothing. They are, in the fullest sense of the phrase, a waste of time. You can miss the shot, die on the beach, get burned by lava, and then get up and get some more potato chips. The games mean nothing.

In a strange parallelism, you can say the same thing about other kinds of entertainment. The sad truth is that entertainment is, by and large, passive. Imagine yourself at an amusement park, for example. All is excitement and thrill and joy and activity, right? Look deeper. The thrill of the newest roller coaster is a totally passive experience. You get strapped in and your heart beats like it is going to escape between your ribs, and the ride creates a surge of adrenaline throughout your body. But nothing in the whole experience depends on you. You are totally passive in this thrill ride. It's pure entertainment without any value to shape your character or hone your skills. Though it feels like a test, it's fake. It is carefully engineered to simulate real experience. The only interactive part of the whole ride is the little booth at the end where you have to decide whether to buy the snapshot that caught you with your mouth open and one hand in the air looking a little like an orangutan ready to scratch.

In their late teen years, my older brothers camped out with a few friends every Memorial Day weekend. The weekend became a yearly tradition for them, an early season ritual. One spring during this campout along the Sand Hill River, my brother Les and my cousin Steve discovered an enormous snapping turtle along the riverbank. Snappers at the best of times are cranky and dangerous, and the jaws that earn them their name can easily remove fingers from the unwary. It's best to leave them alone and go on your way. But this snapper in the trail looked to these young men like a test. All they had for a weapon was Les' hunting knife with a five inch blade. They worked out a plan, and Steve distracted the turtle while Les circled around behind. Using nothing but that knife, Les killed the turtle. They cooked the meat in camp, saved out the shell and put it on an ant mound to clean off the leftover shards of muscle. Les strung the snapper's claws on a leather thong and wore them around his neck, under his shirt, for years. He had passed the test.

A few years later, my mother, who had noticed many times the envious looks I gave Les whenever he pulled his simple snapping turtle claws over his head, got me a necklace of claws. I think they were some kind of crab claws. I have no real idea because I had no part in taking them from whatever creature used them before. I wore them once or twice, then left them laying out in the yard and the dog chewed them up. They carried no weight for me. They were a decoration, not a badge of honor. Les wore claws that connected him to a test, an experience of life and death, a dangerous creature.

Do I have what it takes to kill a snapping turtle with a knife? In today's urban marketplace, it's not something to put on your resume. But a man needs to know he can rise up to a challenge that will cost him more than losing a video game or having a bad week in Fantasy Football. Our world is full of tests, from video games to standardized scholastic tests and their rash of number two pencil-filled ovals. These artificial assessments are not the tests that matter. If you do not risk your blood, your flesh, your well-being, your reputation, it's not a real test. Yet we spend so much of our lives preparing for tests that don't really matter. Is this all there is, to carve your name as high score on a video game? Is it really worth it to win the rat race?

The promotion, the end-of-year bonus, the new car; none of these will satisfy us, at least not for long. Most of the time, deep down, we know we have betrayed our souls to earn these perks. We use the term "human" loosely to speak of a species, but in its origin the word means that we are one with the earth, that we are of the "humus," the soil, that our lives are linked to the dirt and the other creatures that live on the dirt. Being human, in the end, is about being connected. It is a messy, bloody business, this being bound to other creatures. But this is where life happens.

When I was a small child, an old deer head hung in our house. The antlers were heavy and dark. Dad told me it came from the Buck Island Trail up at the Shack. One fall years ago I spent a week at the Shack by myself. The fall was dry enough (miracle of miracles) that I could hike through the peat bogs back into the Buck Island country before freeze-up. Jason joined me for a couple days. We put miles on our feet each day, hunting ruffed grouse and enjoying a gorgeous fall in the woods. The day after Jason left, I walked farther down the Buck Island Trail than I had ever been before. I basked in the glow of hunting the same country Dad had loved so much. One afternoon I cut cross-country around a series of marshes. I stopped to read the fresh tracks along the water's edge. Moose tracks by the dozen, a single bear trail, a handful of whitetails, and many, many fresh wolf prints. I climbed a tree and sat for most of an hour, just looking out and wondering if Dad had sat in any of these same trees. I cut eastward through a stand of poplars and shot a grouse just before I returned to the trail.

The trail of a hunter often takes us into heart-wrenching places, places where we have to step up and do the hard things. This trail will also take you into places of unbelievable beauty and joy that will break your heart if you let it in. It is a trail that may wound us deeply; it is certainly a trail that will test us in the ways that really count. In the testing and the proving, the trying, the failing, the dying and the killing and the living, in the waiting and watching, in the blood and the cold and the long nights, we may find ourselves. We may grow into our identity as human beings.

Summer

Triage

It wasn't my car that hit the doe. But I was there at her death, and complicit in it.

I have hit deer too many times before. A half dozen that I can specifically remember, brakes and adrenaline and dread and sickening thud and danger and blood and death and lasting damage. It is a sad fact of life that deer and vehicles do not coexist well.

But I didn't hit this doe. That happened earlier, and I got drawn into the ending of her pain.

It was a lovely summer day and I had parked my massive water truck along a paved two-lane road in southeastern Minnesota, waiting to refill the spraying rig my partner operates. He called and said, "There's a doe over west on the property line. I called the sheriff's deputy. He'll be here soon." I walked up the road to wait, to give directions, and to assess. Was this really necessary?

In emergency rooms it's called triage, the idea that you have to evaluate the damage in order to give appropriate aid. Often there is a sign on the wall to remind those of us with minor ailments that "the worst go first."

When I first saw her, she was standing fifty yards from the roadway, head down in the young corn, looking for all the world like she was grazing. Maybe it's not so bad, I thought. I've known deer to be hit and bounce back relatively quickly. One December night my daughter and I collided with a nice buck whose skull and antlers shattered my windshield, leaving a silhouette of his profile right in front of the steering wheel in the spiderwebbed glass, inches from my wide eyes. I was doing over fifty miles per hour when we collided, and he took the whole impact to his head. There's no way he could survive, we thought. So after getting safely off to the side of the road and taking a look at the spectacular damage, we went tracking in the fresh snow. We expected to find him dead within a few yards of the road. We saw where he had spun around, fallen, crawled, and fallen again. His tracks described a crazy weave in the clean snow. Then slowly, the weave became a stagger, and the stagger became a walk, and after a quarter mile his tracks merged with a well-traveled trail, and disappeared. We gave up, shaking our heads at the resilience of this buck.

So I watched, and wondered about the doe. Maybe she was just recovering. I worked my way around and noticed, first, that her head never came up. She never looked around, though I was less than fifty yards away in plain sight. She was not alert, a sure sign of trouble for a whitetail. I could see one of her back legs was obviously broken, but that doesn't define things for a deer. There was more wrong. The flies were plaguing her, but her tail never flicked to chase them away. She stood hunched over, head down, staring at but not seeing a spot five feet in front of her. She had bedded down several places here and there, and my eyes teared to think of her agony in lying down and getting up again.

The deputy arrived and we talked briefly about the doe. I hate this part of the job, he said. He took an AR-15 rifle from his truck, loaded it, and walked to within twenty yards of her agony. Her head came up then, slowly, making eye contact with the officer. One quick, precise shot to the head and she fell, twitched twice and was still.

Mercy.

"Thanks for all you do," I said, and he just shook his head. I walked back to my truck.

Ending things can be a hard decision. Ecclesiastes says that "there is a time to die." How to decide when it's time for the death of a deer, a pet, a person, an idea, a relationship, a church? How to do the triage, to weigh treatment options, to opt for compassionate care or a merciful death? Ask any doctor and they will tell you that though there are important guidelines and principles, it's not an easy science.

And beyond science, emotion rises up and threatens to break the levees of our lives, swamping us with fears of guilt and shame. If they unplug life support, does that mean they don't love him anymore? If I file for divorce, does that mean I am a failure? If we vote to close the church, are we dishonoring the generations that built it?

Endings are hard, and discerning how to handle them is harder. Triage is necessary. Discernment is crucial. And we don't always get it right. We don't have the luxury of flying into the future and looking back with 20/20 hindsight that allows us to say, "That was exactly the right decision! Why did I put it off so long?!" No, we live and love and die and grieve in the present, and (this is important) God knows this.

While the people around you may well second-guess your decisions, God never does. He wraps your imperfect discernment, your fears and your hopes, even your failures and mistakes, into his glorious future. He takes the toughest of our endings and brings about the most beautiful resurrections.

In a biblical view, after all, there is no resurrection without death. Be comforted. Grieve. Pray, and make the hard decisions.

Mercy.

Life is in the Blood

Blood is not always your friend.

It was a beautiful late summer day, light breeze and warm sunlight, a few puffy clouds in the sky and temperatures in the mid-70's. It was a Friday, and I had the day off. What could be better?

I writhed in pain on the living room floor. The pain in the back of my head was unbelievable. It felt like one of the vertebrae in my neck had exploded, and every time I turned my head to the side I could hear a wicked crackling sound that felt for all the world like bone fragments grinding over each other. The pain shooting through my skull was making me nauseous. Sweat drenched the rolled up towel I had under the back of my neck in a futile attempt to stabilize whatever had gone wrong.

I learned later that sometime during that quiet, peaceful morning while I lay reading in my hammock or casually checked a couple gopher traps on the edge of my lawn, a tiny blood vessel on the surface of my brain had broken. Blood had leaked into something called the "sub-arachnoid" layer beneath my skull. By the time they got me to the emergency room, the doctor looked at the CAT scan and said, "Whoa, that's a lot of blood." Then he called a helicopter.

When blood stays where it belongs, inside the proper organs and vessels in the body, it is your best friend. The Bible even says that life resides in the blood. But when blood starts to get out of the body, or when it begins to migrate into places in the body where it doesn't belong, it can be a terrible enemy. I found out later that the crackling sensation I'd felt when I turned my head was the volume of blood shifting within the subarachnoid layer surrounding my brain, like water sloshing back and forth within a ziplock bag.

The life is in the blood. In fact, the name the Bible gives to the first man (Adam) is a play on words. "Dam" is the Hebrew word for soil, and "Adamah" is the word for blood. "Adam" is the man who is made of the soil, who has the gift of life coursing through his veins.

That September day on the helicopter, I discovered how thin is the line that separates life from death. Looking out the window at that blue sky, levering myself up on one elbow to take a look out the window at the Mississippi River scooting beneath us (not a bad view), I realized that the clock on my life might be down to just a few minutes. Who knew when something else might give way in my brain? I'd officiated at funerals for people my own age who dropped dead from exactly this kind of a bleed. What could I do? Nothing. I lay back on the gurney and watched the clouds go by out the helicopter window.

Drop back in time a few years. Owen was a tall, lanky Norwegian farmer with a dry voice and a drier sense of humor. As a young man he participated in the invasion of Iwo Jima. He saw things on those beaches that he didn't like to talk about later in life. Decades later, one bitter November Sunday after church he slipped on the ice and broke his hip on the sidewalk. I knelt in the cold wind by his side and covered him with my coat while we waited for the ambulance.

Later I brought communion to Owen in the hospital. He was weak, barely able to swallow the tiny wafer of bread I dipped in wine and slipped between his lips. "Owen, the body of Christ, broken for you. The blood of Christ, shed for you." I laid my hand on his forehead and repeated the ancient words: "May the Lord bless you and keep you. The Lord make his face shine on you and be gracious to you. The Lord lift up his face toward you and give you peace." Owen closed his eyes and slid into a heavy sleep. He died the next day.

A different place, a different time: Sitting on the riverbank behind the funeral home on the banks of the

Mississippi. My daughter Erica is sitting with a few of her friends there on the riverbank, sharing a box of Kleenex. Scotty's body is upstairs in the funeral home, laid out in the coffin surrounded by flowers and a tangle of grieving family and friends. I sit in silence and pain with these teenagers torn by the grief they should not yet know, a grief caused by their friend's suicide. Erica's tears and nose run freely as she turns to me. "Daddy, how do you do this?" she asks. "You do a lot of funerals. How do you do this without going insane?"

Nobody's ever asked me that before. "I guess you learn to grieve," I finally say. "It doesn't get easy, but it gets easier." Great job, Dad.

Erica was only three when we buried my mom. My mother, fifty-seven years old, started having chest pains one afternoon. Mom was the strongest woman I ever knew, strong in every possible way. For more than thirty years she worked the farm with Dad, sorting cattle and driving silage truck with the men, tending her kitchen and preparing meals, shepherding her children. She also worked part time in town at the school. One afternoon, fist clenched over her chest, she stopped in to see Lorraine, the school nurse. Lorraine took one look and called the ambulance.

"Isn't there anything you can do for me?" Mom asked. She lost consciousness in the ambulance and died before they reached the hospital. The doctor said later that she could have been in the emergency room and there would have been nothing the doctors could do. She had an aneurysm in her coronary artery that gave way and she bled out into her chest cavity. Dad called me that night, 1500 miles away. His first words were, "The world ended today."

A few days and a long, difficult drive home later, my brothers and I gathered at Faaberg Lutheran Church. In this church we, along with our two sisters, had been baptized in

Mom's arms. It was the evening before the funeral, and it was just the four of us, the funeral director, and Mom. "Seems fitting," the funeral director observed. "She carried you boys enough times. Now it's your turn to carry her." Together the four of us lifted her casket and slowly climbed the dozen steps into the sanctuary.

Being back in that home country always brings back a flood of memories. Those hills and woods and fields surround my earliest recollections. I remember being six years old, sitting between Kevin and Les, my older brothers, on the front seat of a 1961 Chevy pickup. We were heading out in the early dawn, before school, to check gopher traps on that icy April morning. I caught a gopher in one of my traps but it wasn't dead yet. Kevin showed me how to break the gopher's neck quickly. The gophers were destroying Dad's alfalfa field and needed to be removed, but I hated the act of bringing death to another living thing. I can't count how many lives I've taken since, and I have never, not once, been comfortable with the act of killing. The weight of taking a life is ponderous, even the life of a rodent.

November. Rifle season. A small buck emerged from the woods at dusk, and from my perch in the oak tree on the corner I was able to center the cross-hairs on his chest and take the shot. As the blast exploded from the muzzle of my rifle, he spun and ran back into the woods. The blood trail was clear. It was beginning to snow. I weighed the options, and chose to put my weight on confidence in a solid shot. I followed quickly into the thickening snowflakes rather than risk losing the trail. By the time I found him, he was down to his last one or two breaths. I stood and waited, unwilling to look away from the death that I had caused. This is one of the most horrible and holy moments in my life, this moment of taking the life of another creature, recognizing the blood on my own hands and the responsibility in my gut. I must not, dare not, take this lightly.

Knife out, cutting through the hair and belly skin to remove the entrails, the diaphragm and warm heart and lungs and liver, my nostrils are full of the rich iron-salty smell of blood. I am elbow deep in the reality of my actions. I grieve for my society, for the multitudes who think meat comes from the grocery store and responsibility is something you shoulder in the workplace. Life is so theoretical for so many people. I use the fresh snow to clean my knife and my hands, leaving bright red stains on the ground. The coyotes will be at the gut pile before daylight, and this buck will hang from the big branch on the boxelder tree in my brother's yard for a day before we cut and wrap the meat. My frozen knuckles are a far cry from video game realities where death simply means Game Over. This matters. This blood, this night matters. This life matters.

We desperately want to be idealistic about death. We dress the dead in their best clothes and try to make them look life-like in their expensive coffins. We package meat on pink styrofoam with absorbent padding underneath to soak up any residual blood. What does a flank steak know about blood? It's neatly wrapped in plastic, not messy at all.

After my subarachnoid hemorrhage, I spent fifteen days in the hospital. Several times I thought I would never make it home. This was a different kind of weight to consider, a different responsibility to carry. What had my life been? What could I leave behind? Was that even my business, or was my duty now just to trust that Jesus, who went into death for my sake, who bled out over Roman nails and a Roman spear point, could now take care of me if I had to cross that border?

Over those fifteen days in the hospital I came again and again to the same realization I found on that helicopter ride. It's about trust. You just have to trust. Death will come, or not. Grief will be a constant companion, so you stand up under it. Joy is a reality. So is freedom. All you ever have is this moment. Hold the weight of it in your heart. Carry it like the treasure it is. Sit quiet for a moment. You might feel the beating of your heart. Your blood pumps like life through your veins. Don't waste it.